MW01631286

The Kingdom of God

Bible Storybook

Tyler Van Halteren

Aleksander Jasinski

Text by Tyler Van Halteren
Illustrations by Aleksander Jasinski

First Printing, 2022

Published in Canada by Lithos Kids Ltd.
Printed in China

ISBN:
978-1-989975-13-8 (Hardcover)
9978-1-989975-18-3 (eBook)

Lithos Kids exists to magnify Christ
through biblically faithful
and beautifully crafted books.

Visit our website to learn more:
www.LithosKids.com

Also available from Lithos Kids:
Little Pilgrim's Big Journey, Part I & II

Dedication

To my mom, Lynn Van Halteren,
who has always been my greatest example
of the King's steadfast love and faithfulness.

This Book Belongs To:

Rejoice greatly, O daughter of Zion!
Shout aloud, O daughter of Jerusalem!
Behold, your king is coming to you;
righteous and having salvation is he,
humble and mounted on a donkey,
on a colt, the foal of a donkey.

Zechariah 9:9

Table of Contents

Introduction

In the Old Testament, we see God's glorious plan to establish his kingdom on earth. But we also see how people continue to rebel against God's reign and how God's kingdom is ruined by sin. The great question we are left with is: how can God's kingdom be restored to earth?

The answer is found in the promised King. All of the Old Testament looks towards a Savior who will come to fulfill God's covenants and make a way for God's people to enter into God's kingdom.

The Gospel of Matthew begins with these words: "The book of the genealogy of Jesus Christ, the son of David, the son of Abraham." Jesus is the one all the prophets were waiting for! He is our promised Savior, our great High Priest, our perfect Sacrifice, and our faithful King. Where all others failed, Jesus was victorious! Jesus is the only one who can restore God's kingdom to this earth.

What is God's kingdom? In this book we summarize it this way:

God's presence
with God's people
in God's place
through God's promises.

A Note to Parents

There are many Bibles for children available today with many different aims. This storybook Bible has five specific aims:

1. To faithfully retell the story of redemption, while focusing on the central theme of the kingdom of God and the importance of covenants.

2. To show how all of Scripture points to Jesus. Each chapter focuses on the longing and need for the promised Savior to come. Our hope and prayer is that by doing so, children will grasp the glory of the gospel from an early age.

3. To follow the original meaning and intent of each story. God's Word is powerful to shape and transform lives, while our words will pass away like dust. While this book can never replace the Bible, we hope it will help prepare your children for a lifetime of reading and studying God's Word.

4. To create a storybook Bible that children can grow into, rather than grow out of. Our hope is that the vivid illustrations will help even the youngest children follow along, while the depth and clarity of the words will encourage them even more as they grow older.

5. To help your family engage deeper with biblical truths. Each chapter begins with verse references, and concludes with a short study guide with summaries, questions, gospel glimpses, and prayers.

Our ultimate prayer and hope is that this book will lead you and your children into a greater love for the King of kings and Lord of lords.

"To the King of the ages, immortal, invisible, the only God, be honor and glory forever and ever. Amen." (1 Timothy 1:17)

Chapter 1:
The King with Us

Bible References:

Matthew 1, Luke 1-2

For thousands of years, God had promised his people that he would send a Savior. God promised Adam and Eve that one of their offspring would crush the head of the serpent. God promised Abraham and Sarah that one of their children would bring blessing to all nations.

God promised David that one of his sons would reign on his throne forever.

Many people forgot God's promises, but some still waited and longed and hoped for this King to come. They had to wait a long time. It had been four hundred years since a prophet had spoken.

At last, the time had come. A new beginning was about to begin. The long-awaited King was about to arrive! How would God announce this good news to the world?

An angel named Gabriel appeared and spoke to a young woman who lived in Nazareth: "Fear not, Mary. You will have a son, and you will call him Jesus. He will be great and will be called the Son of the Most High. The Lord God will give him the throne of his father David, and he will reign forever over the house of Jacob. Of his kingdom there will be no end."

Mary was amazed! She sang out, "My soul magnifies the Lord. He has helped his servant Israel. God has remembered his mercy, as he promised to Abraham and his offspring forever."

Just as Gabriel promised, this baby began to grow in Mary's womb. This was no ordinary child—he was formed by the Holy Spirit. This fulfilled a prophecy from Isaiah:

"The virgin will conceive and bear a son,
and will be called Immanuel, which means,
'God with us.'"

In those days, Caesar Augustus was the emperor of Rome
and the world's most powerful ruler. Caesar reigned over many nations, including Israel, and he wanted to know just how great his kingdom was. Caesar commanded everyone to register their family in their hometowns.

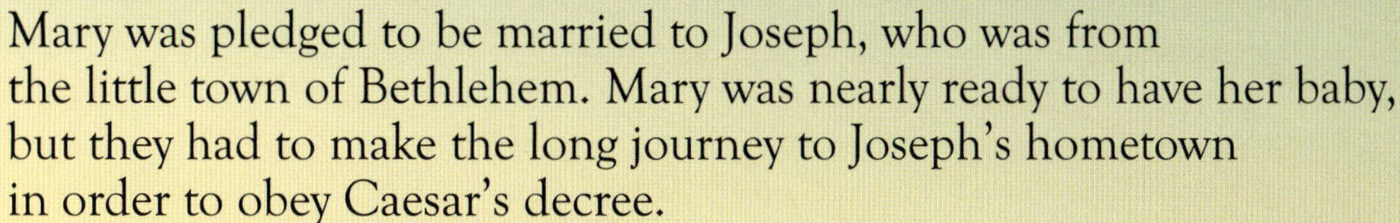

Mary was pledged to be married to Joseph, who was from the little town of Bethlehem. Mary was nearly ready to have her baby, but they had to make the long journey to Joseph's hometown in order to obey Caesar's decree.

Even though this seemed like bad timing, God had a plan that was far greater than Caesar's plan. Bethlehem was the same town where King David was born— and many years before, God had promised that this was where the promised King would be born.

Joseph and Mary arrived in Bethlehem just in time for Mary to give birth.
The promised Savior was about to enter the world!
This was the moment that Israel had waited thousands of years for.
The streets should have been full of rejoicing and celebration!

But Bethlehem's streets were full of chaos and confusion. The town was so busy that Mary and Joseph couldn't find a room where they could stay. Even in this, God had a plan.

Instead of announcing the birth of Jesus to great kings and princes, God announced it to lowly shepherds. An angel of the Lord appeared to these shepherds—and they were terrified!

The angel said to the shepherds, "Do not fear! I bring you good news of great joy that will be for all people. The promised Savior has been born in the city of David." Suddenly a great multitude of angels appeared and praised God by singing, "Glory to God in the highest, and on earth peace to those on whom his favor rests!"

Where would this child be born? Not in a palace or a grand castle.
He had to sleep in a manger. This highest of kings had the lowest of births.
But this was no mistake—God's kingdom isn't like other kingdoms.
God chooses to use the weak and lowly of this world to display his greatness.

The shepherds hurried to meet this new King. They told Mary and Joseph everything the angels had said. When Mary and Joseph heard their story, they were filled with great joy. They knew that God was fulfilling the promises he made to Israel. Here was the child that Adam, Abraham, David, and the prophets had been waiting for. In that little stable lay the promised Savior—Immanuel, "God with us!"

The King with Us

God's Presence: The birth of Jesus is the greatest expression of God's presence with his people. In the Old Testament, God lived among the Israelites in the tabernacle and temple, now God's Son has come to dwell with humans. Jesus is Immanuel, God with us.

God's People: God reveals the birth of Jesus to shepherds. God could have revealed himself to kings, princes, and powerful people, but instead he announces the birth of Jesus to lowly people.

God's Place: Bethlehem was the place where King David was born, and Jesus is born there to fulfill prophecies about the promised King. Though Caesar, the emperor of Rome, is in control of the land of Israel, God is still at work in this land.

God's Promise: Through Jesus' birth, we see God's covenant promises fulfilled. Jesus is the offspring of the woman who would crush the serpent, the offspring of Abraham who would bless all nations, and the offspring of David who would reign forever.

Questions

1. How did Jesus fulfill God's promises to Abraham and David?
2. Why did God announce Jesus' birth to shepherds?
3. What does the name 'Immanuel' mean? Why is that important?

Gospel Glimpse

Jesus came into this world as fully God and fully man (Colossians 1:15). He is the fulfillment of God's promises, and demonstrated just how far God would go to dwell with his people (Isaiah 7:14).

Prayer

We praise you, our Lord, for your perfect plan. Thank you for sending Jesus to dwell with us, so we can dwell with you forever.

Chapter 2:
Let Earth Receive the King!

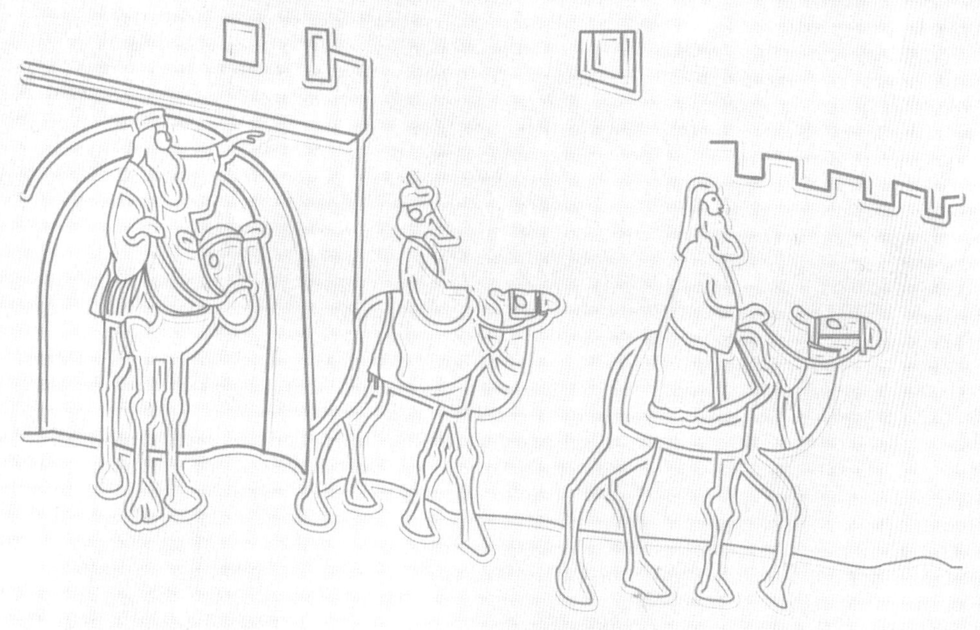

Bible References:

Matthew 2, Luke 2:22-38

The shepherds weren't the only people who came looking for this King. Wise men traveled from far in the east to visit the city of Jerusalem.

While many of the Jews didn't know and didn't care that their promised King had come, these wise men left their homes and made a long journey to seek him

They came to the palace of King Herod, the ruler of Jerusalem, and asked him, "Where is the one who was born King of the Jews? We saw his star rising in the sky, and have come to worship him."

Herod was confused and angry by what these wise men told him. He thought he was the king of the Jews! Later, in secret, he asked some Jewish leaders, "Where is the promised Savior to be born?"

They told him about this prophecy God had made:
"A ruler will come from Bethlehem, in the land of Judah.
He will be like a shepherd to the people of Israel."

So Herod sent the wise men to Bethlehem. He told them,
"When you find this child, let me know, so I can come and worship him."
But what Herod really wanted was to kill this child.

The wise men continued their journey. When they saw the star, they were full of great joy. God had placed this special star in the sky to lead them to the promised King.

Herod did not want this newborn King to take over his kingdom.
If the wise men didn't return and tell him where this child was,
he was ready to send soldiers into Bethlehem to kill every baby there.
He didn't care about God's kingdom; he wanted all the power himself.
But God would protect Jesus from Herod's evil plans.

When the wise men saw Jesus, they worshiped him.
They knew that Jesus was the true King, and they gave him costly gifts—gold, and frankincense, and myrrh.

Gold was a gift for royalty. Frankincense was used to worship God in the temple. And myrrh was used to prepare bodies for burial. The wise men's gifts were a powerful picture of who Jesus was—the King of kings, the Son of God, and the perfect sacrifice for our sins.

Joseph and Mary went to dedicate Jesus at the temple. They met a man named Simeon who was waiting for God's promised Savior to bring God's kingdom to earth. When Simeon saw Jesus, he praised God and said, "Now my eyes have seen God's salvation! He will be a light to the nations and glory to Israel."

An older woman named Anna was also there. When she saw Jesus, she gave thanks to God. She told everyone, "God has come to redeem Jerusalem!"

Jesus had come to bring God's kingdom to earth.
But not everyone received him with joy.
Some would welcome and worship him,
while others would reject him and walk away.
Some would rejoice to see God's promised King,
while others would seek their own kingdoms.

Let Earth Receive the King!

God's Presence: Jesus' arrival is the moment that Israel had been waiting thousands of years for. But when Jesus comes to dwell with his people, some receive him with joy and some reject him in pride.

God's People: The wise men travel from the East to see the promised King. They demonstrate that God's people aren't limited to just Israel, but to all who will receive the King with joy. Unlike the wise men, Herod rejects God's king and demonstrates he is not one of God's people.

God's Place: Herod reigns over Jerusalem as the king of the Jews, but he was not seeking God's kingdom. Herod sought to kill Jesus, and eventually sent soldiers into Bethlehem to murder all children under two years old. Because of this, Mary and Joseph had to flee to Egypt.

God's Promise: Jesus fulfills all of God's promises and prophecies about the promised King. He will bring God's blessing to the nations and God's salvation to the ends of the earth.

Questions

1. Who received King Jesus with joy in this story?
2. Who rejected King Jesus? Why?
3. What do the wise men teach us about God's plan for the nations?

Gospel Glimpse

John 1:11-12 says, "He came to his own, and his own people did not receive him. But to all who did receive him, who believed in his name, he gave the right to become children of God." The most important decision anyone will ever make is whether to receive or reject Jesus as their King.

Prayer

O God, help our hearts to receive Jesus as Savior and follow him as King. Thank you for the hope, peace, joy, and love that are found in you alone.

Chapter 3: The Kingdom of Heaven is Near

Bible References:

Matthew 3-4, Luke 3-4

God chose a man named John to prepare the way for the promised King. John lived in the wilderness and ate locusts and honey for food. He seemed like a strange messenger for God to use, but John's words were powerful. He called out to everyone, "Turn from your sin, for the kingdom of heaven is coming!"

Hundreds of years before, the prophet Isaiah spoke about John. Isaiah said John would be like a voice crying in the wilderness: "Prepare the way for the Lord!"

Everyone went out to listen to John, and many were baptized by him in the Jordan River. Some thought John might be the promised Savior, but John told them, "I baptize you with water, but one who is greater than I is coming. I am not even worthy to untie the straps of his sandals. He will baptize you with the Holy Spirit."

The Pharisees and Jewish leaders didn't like John, and they didn't want to get baptized. Their hearts weren't ready to receive the promised Savior.

When Jesus came to the Jordan River, John declared,
"Behold, the Lamb of God, who takes away the sin of the world!"

Jesus wanted to be baptized by John, but John told him,
"I need to be baptized by you! Why do you come to be baptized by me?"
Jesus answered, "Let it be so, for I am here to do all that is right."
So John dipped Jesus under the water.

When Jesus came up, the heavens were opened, and the Spirit of God came down upon him like a dove! A voice from heaven said, "This is my beloved Son! With him I am well pleased."

Jesus was anointed by the Holy Spirit to do everything God the Father prepared for him. Jesus truly was the promised Savior!

After his baptism, Jesus was led by God's Spirit into the wilderness.
Satan came there and tried to tempt Jesus to sin,
just as the serpent had tempted Adam and Eve in Eden.
But Jesus wasn't in a beautiful garden—he was in a desert.
Satan told him, "If you are the Son of God, tell these stones
to become loaves of bread."

Jesus answered, “It is written, ‘Man shall not live by bread alone, but by every word that comes from the mouth of God.’”

Long ago, when the Israelites were in the wilderness for forty years, they complained and grumbled to God. But even when Jesus hadn’t eaten for forty days, he trusted his Father in this time of testing.

Then Satan took Jesus to a high mountain and showed him all the kingdoms of the world and their glory. Satan told him, "All these I will give you, if you fall down and worship me."

Jesus answered, "It is written, 'You shall worship the Lord your God and serve him only.'" Satan was trying to tempt Jesus to take the easy road to receive a kingdom, but Jesus didn't listen. Jesus was seeking God's true and eternal kingdom.

Finally Satan took Jesus to the top of the temple and said, "If you are God's Son, throw yourself down from here. For it is written, 'God will send his angels to help you.'" Jesus answered, "It is written, 'You shall not put the Lord your God to the test.' Be gone, Satan!"

Satan tried everything to defeat Jesus, but he could not.
Jesus was victorious! He did not fall into sin,
as so many of God's people had done in the past.
At last, the promised King who could defeat the serpent had come!

Jesus went to Nazareth, the town where he was raised.
He went to the synagogue and read these words from the scroll of Isaiah:
"The Spirit of the Lord is upon me, because he has anointed me
to proclaim good news to the poor. He sent me to proclaim freedom
to the captives and give sight to the blind, to set the oppressed free,
and to proclaim the year of the Lord's favor."

Jesus told everyone in the synagogue:
"Today this scripture has been fulfilled in your hearing."
He was the promised Savior who all the prophets had spoken about!

After all these years of waiting for God's promises to come true,
how would these people respond to Jesus?
Some of his listeners were glad to hear his words!
But others said, "Isn't he only the son of Joseph?"
They knew his family, and watched him grow up.
They didn't really believe that Jesus was the Son of God.

People in Nazareth had heard about Jesus's miracles, but they didn't believe. They demanded that he prove that he was sent from God and do a miracle for them.

Jesus told them, "No prophet is accepted in his hometown." Many years before, the prophet Elijah had also been rejected by his own people. Jesus told how Elijah did not perform miracles in his hometown because of people's unbelief. Instead, Elijah went out to heal and help people from other nations.

Everyone in the Nazareth synagogue became angry when Jesus said this. They thought they didn't need any help from Jesus. They made him leave. They even brought him to a cliff and tried to push him off!

After all these years, Israel's heart was so hard that they rejected their promised Savior! Like sheep, God's people had gone astray, but like a good shepherd, Jesus would bring them back. Jesus miraculously walked through this crowd and wasn't hurt. They could not take Jesus's life, but one day he would freely give up his life to save his people from their sin.

The Kingdom of Heaven is Near

God's Presence: When Jesus begins his ministry, he announces, "The Kingdom of God is near." He is declaring that he will bring God's presence to reign over the world.

God's People: When Jesus announces he is the promised Savior in his hometown, he is rejected by his own people. This is a surprising twist to the story, as the people who should be most excited for his arrival become greatly angered with him and even try to throw him off a cliff.

God's Place: Jesus is bringing the kingdom of Heaven down to earth. He shows us that God's plan is not just to reign over Israel, but over the whole world.

God's Promise: By overcoming Satan in the wilderness, Jesus demonstrates that he is the promised offspring of Adam who will defeat the serpent. Jesus quotes Isaiah 61 and announces he is the promised Savior who will fulfill all of God's promises.

Questions

1. How did John the Baptist prepare the way for Jesus?
2. What did Satan promise to Jesus? How did Jesus overcome?
3. Who rejected Jesus in this chapter? Why?

Gospel Glimpse

Jesus is the sinless lamb of God who takes away the sins of the world (John 1:29). Jesus is the promised offspring who would defeat the Serpent (Genesis 3:15). Where all others failed, Jesus succeeded!

Prayer

Our Father in heaven, holy is your name. May your kingdom come, and your will be done, on earth as it is in heaven.

Chapter 4:
Following the King

Bible References:

Matthew 16-17, Luke 9

In those days, Jewish teachers would seek disciples
who would follow and learn from them.
When Jesus looked for his disciples, he didn't go to the best schools
or the wealthiest parts of town—instead he went to a lake.
He entered the boat of a fisherman named Peter
and said, "Go out to the deep water and let out your nets."

Peter answered, "We worked all night,
and we caught nothing.
But at your word, I will cast out my nets."

When they lifted up the nets, there were so many fish that the nets started to break. They had to call their friends for help. Together, they filled two boats full of fish.

When Peter saw this, he fell down at Jesus's knees. He said, "Go away from me, for I am a sinful man." Jesus said to him, "Do not be afraid. From now on, you will be fishing for men." That day Peter and his friends left everything and followed after Jesus.

If calling fishermen to follow him wasn't strange enough, Jesus also called Matthew, a tax collector, to be his disciple. Most Jews hated tax collectors, because they worked for the Romans and took money from their own people.

But Jesus was calling Matthew to a new future in the kingdom of God. When Jesus said, "Follow me," Matthew immediately left everything behind and followed him.

Matthew made a great feast at his house. Many tax collectors and other people joined the feast with Jesus. The Pharisees and religious leaders grumbled. They said to Jesus, "Why do you eat and drink with these sinners?"

Jesus answered, "Those who are healthy don't need a doctor, but the sick do. I haven't come to call people who think they are righteous, but people who know they are sinners." Jesus was forming a new kingdom that was nothing like what the Pharisees expected.

Once, while Jesus was eating a meal with a Pharisee, a woman rushed in and fell at Jesus's feet. She was crying, and began wiping Jesus's feet with her hair. She broke open a bottle of expensive ointment and anointed his feet with oil.

The Pharisee was shocked. He thought to himself, "If this man was a prophet, he would know what sort of woman this is. She is a sinner!"

Jesus told the Pharisee a story: "Two people owed a man money. One owed five hundred denarii, and the other owed only fifty. When these two couldn't pay the money back, the man canceled their debt. Which one do you think will love him more?"

The Pharisee answered, "The one who had the bigger debt."

"You are right," Jesus said. "Do you see this woman? When I entered your house, you gave me no water for my feet, but she has wet them with her tears. You did not anoint my head, but she has anointed my feet with oil. The person who is forgiven little, loves little."

Then Jesus said to the woman, "Your sins are forgiven. Your faith has saved you. Go in peace." And everyone at the table wondered about Jesus: "Who is this? This man even forgives sins!"

Jesus chose twelve disciples to follow him and stay close to him,
much like God had chosen the twelve tribes of Israel to be his people.
Jesus was forming a new people to be part of his kingdom.
Jesus revealed many things to his disciples that other people did not get to hear.

As they traveled, Jesus asked them, "Who do people say I am?"
His disciples answered, "Some say you are John the Baptist,
others say Elijah, or Jeremiah, or one of the prophets."
"But who do you say that I am?" Jesus asked.

Peter answered, “You are the Messiah, the Son of the living God!”

Jesus told Peter, “Blessed are you! For no human could reveal this to you, but only my Father who is in heaven.”

Many people thought that when the promised King came,
he would give the Israelites victory over their enemies, and rule over all the world.
But Jesus taught his disciples something else. Jesus told them,
“The Son of Man must suffer many things. I will be rejected and killed,
and on the third day be raised.”

Following Jesus would not be an easy road to an earthly kingdom;
it would be a difficult road to an everlasting kingdom.
Jesus told his disciples, "If anyone would follow me, he must deny himself and take up his cross every day. For whoever tries to save their life will lose it, but whoever loses their life for my sake will save it. What does it profit a person to gain the whole world but lose his soul?"

Jesus wanted his disciples to know that his suffering would lead to a greater glory. He took three of his disciples up on a mountain. As Jesus prayed, he was transfigured. His face shone like the sun, and his clothes became white as light.

The three disciples saw his glory,and they were amazed.
A cloud appeared around them,
and they heard a voice speak out:
"This is my beloved Son,
with whom I am well pleased.
Listen to him."

Moses and Elijah also appeared. They were two of the greatest men in the Old Testament—but someone greater had arrived. God gave Moses the law, and Elijah was a prophet, but the law and all the prophets were pointing to Jesus.

Following the King

God's Presence: As God displayed his presence to Moses and Elijah on a mountain, Jesus displays his glory to his three disciples on a mountain. When Jesus is transfigured, he is demonstrating that he is sent from God and is bringing God's presence to earth.

God's People: Jesus calls many unlikely people to be his disciples. Jesus chooses twelve disciples, as a reflection of the twelve tribes of Israel. He is forming a new people of God who will bring God's blessing to the world.

God's Place: Jesus calls his disciples to take up their cross and follow him. The road to God's kingdom would not be easy, but costly. God's kingdom would not come on earth immediately, but through great suffering.

God's Promise: On the mountain, Moses and Elijah speak with Jesus about the great Exodus he would achieve in Jerusalem. In the first Exodus, Moses delivered Israel from slavery in Egypt and brought them to the Promised Land. In this New Exodus, Jesus was going to deliver his people from slavery to sin and bring them into his eternal Kingdom.

Questions

1. What kind of people did Jesus call to be his disciples?
2. Why did Jesus choose twelve disciples?
3. Would it be easy or hard to follow Jesus? Why?

Gospel Glimpse

Jesus calls people from all types of backgrounds to follow him. The beauty of the Gospel is that God's grace reaches to even the worst sinners. Jesus came to "seek and save the lost" (Luke 19:10).

Prayer

Lord, thank you that you came for sinners like us. Help us to follow you when life is easy and when life is hard.

Chapter 5: The King's Power

Bible References:

Matthew 8-9, Luke 8, John 11

Jesus told his disciples, "I have come for this purpose: to proclaim the kingdom of God." While Jesus travelled and preached, he also showed his power and kindness as the promised King. Jesus had power over all kinds of sickness.

Once, when Jesus was walking through a crowd, a woman came behind him and touched the edge of his robe. This woman had been very sick for twelve years. She spent all her money seeking help from doctors, but no one could heal her. She was desperate and ashamed—and Jesus was her only hope. The moment she touched Jesus's robe, she was healed! Jesus told her, "Daughter, your faith has made you well. Go in peace."

At another time, Jesus was teaching in a house where a great crowd gathered. A paralyzed man came to be healed by Jesus. His friends carried him on a bed.

The room was so crowded that there was no way to get in, but they knew Jesus was their only hope. So they opened up the roof and lowered the paralyzed man down to Jesus. When Jesus saw their faith, he said, “Rise and walk.” And the man was healed!

Jesus had power over evil spirits.
Even the demons knew Jesus was the promised King.
They called out to him, "Have you come to destroy us?
We know who you are–you are the Son of God!"

Jesus came to a place where he met a man who had many demons.
This man lived outside a city among the tombs. People in that city
were so scared of the man that they sometimes had to chain him up.
But he was so powerful he would break out of the chains.
No one could control him or calm him down.

When the man saw Jesus, he cried out,
"What have you to do with me, Jesus, Son of the Most High God?"
Then the demons begged Jesus not to send them into judgment.

With a word, Jesus commanded the demons to leave the man,
and he was freed!

Jesus had power over all of his creation. When he was in a boat with his disciples, a great storm arose. But Jesus wasn't afraid—in fact, Jesus was sleeping. His disciples panicked and woke him and shouted, "Master! We are going to die!"

Jesus stood and rebuked the wind and the waves. He said, "Peace, be still!"
Suddenly the storm stopped, and the waters became calm.
The disciples were terrified and amazed. They said to each other,
"Who is this, that even the winds and the waves obey his command?"

Jesus had power over sickness, evil spirits, and storms.
But did Jesus even have power over death?
Some of his disciples weren't sure.

Two of his followers were Mary and Martha. They sent for Jesus and said, "Lazarus, our brother, is very sick." Jesus waited two days and went to visit them.

When Jesus arrived, Lazarus had already died. Martha came to Jesus and said, "Lord, if you were here my brother wouldn't have died."

Jesus told her, "I am the resurrection and the life.
Whoever believes in me, even when they die, will live again."

Then Mary fell at Jesus' feet and began crying.
And Jesus wept with her.

When the people saw Jesus crying, they said,
"Look how he loved Lazarus!"
Others said, "If he opened the eyes of the blind,
why couldn't he heal his friend?"

Jesus came to the cave where they had buried the body of Lazarus. Jesus said, "Take away the stone." Martha was confused. She told Jesus, "Lord, there will be a terrible odor. Lazarus has been dead four days already."

Jesus told Martha, "If you believe, you will see the glory of God." Then Jesus called to the tomb, "Lazarus, come out!"

And Lazarus came out! Everyone was astonished, and news of this miracle spread throughout all the towns.

The true King had come to reverse the curse of sin. Jesus was showing what life in the kingdom would be like—with no more sickness, or sorrow, or danger, or death. He cleansed the unclean, he welcomed the outcasts, and he defeated the powers of darkness.

He was fixing the broken things in this world, because in God's kingdom, nothing is broken anymore. One day, Jesus will return to defeat death once and for all, and he will wipe away everyone's tears.

The King's Power

God's Presence: Jesus shows God's power as he heals the sick, calms storms, casts out demons, and raises the dead. Jesus has authority over all things, and brings God's healing presence into the world.

God's People: Jesus shows that even people considered unclean are welcome to be part of his people. He heals many people that the religious leaders would never touch, and calls them to place their faith in him.

God's Place: The temple was a holy place because God's holy presence was within it. Unclean people were not able to enter. Jesus shows that God's reign extends beyond the temple into the whole earth, and foreshadows how God will restore the world.

God's Promise: It was promised that the Savior would bring healing and restoration to his people. Jesus fulfills all of God's promises and makes a way for even outcasts to come into his kingdom.

Questions

1. Can you list three things that Jesus had power over?
2. What did demons and unclean spirits say to Jesus?
3. How did Jesus demonstrate God's kingdom?

Gospel Glimpse

Many of the people Jesus healed were outcasts who were considered unclean by the Jewish leaders, but Jesus made them clean. In God's kingdom, there is no more death, sickness, or sadness.

Prayer

Almighty God, we see your power displayed throughout all history. Thank you for displaying your grace and goodness through Jesus.

Chapter 6: The Upside-Down Kingdom

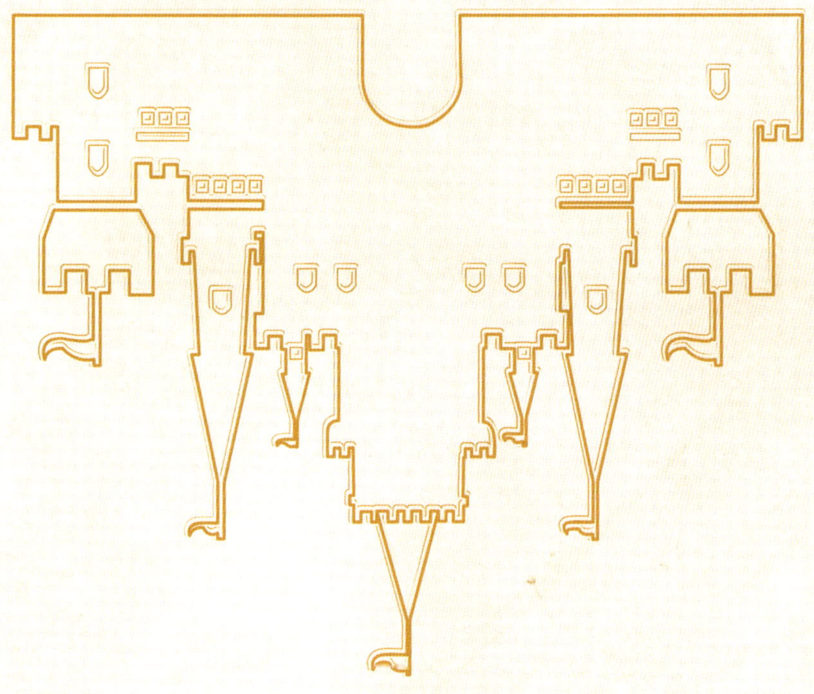

Bible References:

Matthew 5-7, Matthew 21, Luke 18

During his three years of ministry, Jesus went through many towns and villages, calling out to people, "Turn from your sin, the kingdom of God is near!" Jesus wanted to prepare them to receive God's promises. He wanted them to understand what it means to be citizens of God's kingdom.

God's kingdom isn't like kingdoms of the world, which belong to the strong and powerful. Jesus taught that God's kingdom is an upside-down kingdom, which belongs to the gentle and the merciful.

Jesus wasn't like any of the kings of this world.
Most kings are rich and live in palaces or castles,
but Jesus had little money and no home.
Jesus was giving his followers an example
of what it means to seek God's kingdom.

Jesus told them:
"Look at the birds–see how your heavenly Father feeds them.
And look at the flowers in the field–see how God clothes them with beauty.
Your heavenly Father knows what you need. Seek first his kingdom
and his righteousness, and all these things will be added to you as well."

Jesus often spoke to the crowds in parables
to explain what his kingdom was like.
Jesus told them, "The kingdom of heaven is like a grain of mustard seed.
It's the smallest of seeds, but when it grows it's larger than all the garden plants."

God's kingdom may seem small, while the world's kingdoms seem so powerful–
but one day God's kingdom will fill the whole earth.

Jesus also said, "The kingdom of heaven is like treasure hidden in a field, which a man found and covered up. Then in his joy he goes and sells all that he has and buys that field."

Jesus taught his followers that God's kingdom is the only treasure worth seeking. It can never fade or be taken away.

While many kingdoms are formed by war and violence,
Jesus taught that his kingdom would be built on peace and forgiveness.
So Jesus told his disciples to pray like this:

"Our Father in heaven, holy is your name. May your kingdom come and your will be done, on earth as it is in heaven. Give us this day our daily bread, and forgive us our debts, as we forgive our debtors. Lead us not into temptation, but deliver us from evil."

Jesus' disciples didn't always understand his upside-down kingdom. One day, they asked him, "Who is the greatest in the kingdom of God?"

Jesus called a child close to him and said to his disciples, "Whoever becomes humble like a child will be greatest in my kingdom." Jesus taught his disciples that his kingdom can't be earned or achieved, but is freely given and received with child-like faith.

Another time, many parents brought their children and babies to Jesus. They wanted him to pray for these little ones and bless them. The disciples rebuked these people and told them to go away. They didn't want the children to bother Jesus.

But Jesus welcomed these children and took them into his arms. He said, "Let the children come, do not send them away. For the kingdom of God belongs to people who are like these little children."

Jesus' teaching surprised many people. But one of the most surprising things happened when Jesus entered the temple.

This was where Jewish people could come to bring sacrifices to God and worship him. When Jesus came in, he didn't find it full of people worshiping—it was full of merchants selling things!

As Jesus had flipped their expectations of the kingdom of God, he flipped their tables. He dumped their money on the floor and told the merchants, "My house shall be called a house of prayer for all nations, but you have made it a den of thieves!"

Jesus was showing that no one can buy or earn their way into God's kingdom. He had come to make a way for all people to freely receive God's grace.

The Upside-Down Kingdom

God's Presence: Jesus brings God's presence in ways that often surprise people. When Jesus is approached by mothers and children, his disciples try to send them away. But Jesus welcomes them and blesses them.

God's People: In the Sermon on the Mount, Jesus teaches that those who are truly citizens of God's kingdom are meek, humble, and merciful. Jesus teaches his disciples that they must become humble and lowly like children.

God's Place: When Jesus enters the temple, he confronts the sin of the merchants who are cheating people for their offerings. The temple is supposed to be the place where God's people come to worship him, but they have turned it into a den of thieves.

God's Promise: Jesus came to welcome people from all nations into his kingdom. While many Jews thought that God would only bless Israel, or that the best places in God's kingdom were reserved for religious leaders, Jesus flipped their expectations.

Questions

1. What does it mean to be a citizen of God's kingdom?
2. How did Jesus respond when children came to him?
3. Why did Jesus flip the tables in the Temple?

Gospel Glimpse

Jesus taught his disciples that his kingdom isn't something that can be earned or achieved, but is something that is given and received (Ephesians 2:8-9). God's kingdom is a gift of God's grace to be received with childlike faith (Mark 10:15).

Prayer

We praise you, O God, that your ways are higher than our ways. You choose the weak and foolish things of the world to shame the strong.

Chapter 7: The Humble King

Bible References:

Matthew 21, Luke 22

After three years of ministry, Jesus made his triumphal entry into Jerusalem! He didn't enter on a royal horse, or in kingly robes. He came riding on a donkey. This fulfilled a prophecy made about the promised King:
"Say to the daughter of Zion, 'Behold, your King is coming to you, humble and mounted on a donkey.'"

Many people placed their cloaks on the road. Others waved palm branches. The crowd followed him and shouted, "Hosanna to the Son of David! Blessed is the King who comes in the name of the Lord! Hosanna in the highest!"

The word *Hosanna* means, "Please save us!" The people knew that the long-awaited Savior had come! Everyone was rejoicing– everyone except for the Jewish leaders. They were angry. They didn't think they needed saving.

Later that week, on Passover night, Jesus met with his disciples in an upper room.
Because the city streets were full of dirt, and everyone's feet got dirty,
it was normal for the lowest servant to wash the feet of guests.
But which of the disciples would take this lowly role?

To their surprise, Jesus laid aside his robes
and began washing the feet of his disciples!

This humble King had come down from heaven.
He laid aside his glory and came to serve his people.
No king in all of history had ever stooped this low.

But those disciples' feet weren't the only thing that needed washing. Their hearts were full of sin. Jesus would stoop even lower to make a way for their hearts to be cleansed as well.

That night, Jesus wanted to share the Passover meal with his disciples, and he would do it in a surprising new way. The Jews celebrated Passover every year—to remember the day when God saved Israel from slavery and brought them out of Egypt.

As the disciples ate this meal, Jesus broke bread and passed it to them, saying, "Take and eat this bread. This is my body." Then he took a cup, and gave it to them, saying, "This cup is the new covenant in my blood, which is poured out for you. I will not drink of this cup again until I drink it with you in my Father's kingdom."

Jesus was teaching them that he would become the Passover lamb. Just as the blood of the lamb saved the Israelites from death, Jesus would die to save his people from their sins.

When they finished the Passover meal, Jesus took his disciples to a garden called Gethsemane. Jesus went by himself and fell on his face and prayed:
"Father, if you are willing, remove this cup from me.
Yet not my will, but yours, be done."

Jesus knew he was going to the cross.
But it wasn't the physical suffering that he most feared.
What Jesus dreaded was the cup of God's righteous anger against sin.
Jesus had never sinned, but his people had sinned many, many times.
He would drink this cup for his people to pay the penalty for their sin.

Jesus prayed three times, asking God
if there was any other way for his people to be saved.
But there was no other way.

When Jesus finished praying, he found his disciples sleeping.
He told them, "Rise and pray, that you may not enter into temptation."
Just then, some Jewish leaders brought soldiers to arrest Jesus.

Jesus said to them, "Am I a robber, that you have come out
with swords and clubs? When I was with you day after day in the temple,
you did not arrest me. But this is your hour and the power of darkness."

Jesus was the light of the world. He was the Savior who had been promised for thousands of years, but the leaders of Israel were so blind they couldn't see that he was the true light. They hated his light, because it revealed their sin. They didn't want God's kingdom to come; they wanted to build their own kingdom.

The Humble King

God's Presence: Many thought that when the Promised Savior came, he would come in might and power. But Jesus came in humility and weakness. We see this as he rides into Jerusalem on a donkey and washes his disciples' feet.

God's People: While the crowd rejoices and praises Jesus, the Pharisees and religious leaders make plans to kill Jesus. While the Pharisees claim to serve God, they demonstrate they are not God's people.

God's Place: Jesus came into Jerusalem as a declaration that he is the King of Israel. While he is received like a king by the people, he is then treated like a thief and a robber by the religious leaders.

God's Promise: Jesus shares the Passover meal with his disciples and tells them he is about to make a new covenant in his blood. This is the fulfillment of many Old Testament prophecies and promises.

Questions

1. How do we see Jesus' humility in this chapter?
2. What is the significance of the Passover meal?
3. Why was Jesus grieved in the garden of Gethsemane?

Gospel Glimpse

Jesus laid aside his glory and came into this world to humbly serve his people (Philippians 2:6-8). Jesus would step down even lower and offer himself as a sacrifice for sin (Matthew 20:28).

Prayer

Thank you, Lord Jesus, for laying aside your glory and becoming a servant. May you be high and exalted in our lives.

Chapter 8: Crowning the King

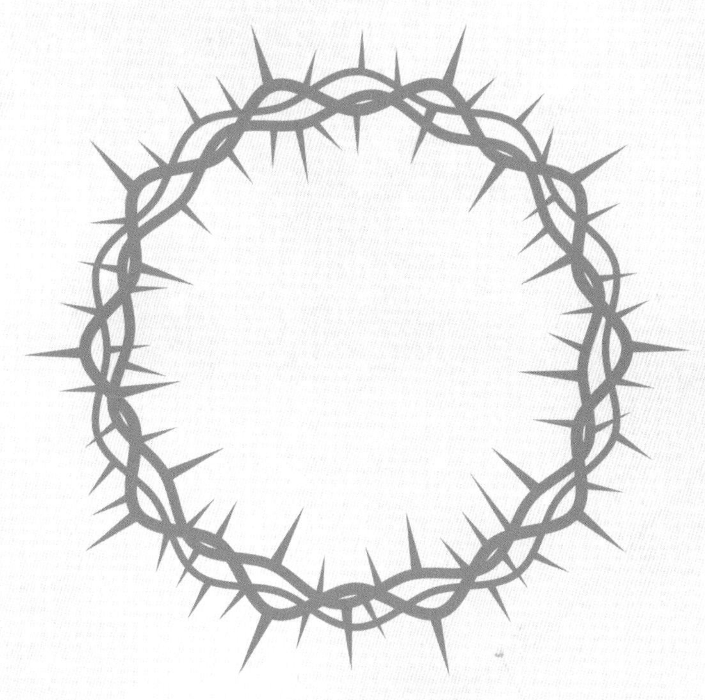

Bible References:
Matthew 27, Luke 23

The Jewish leaders brought Jesus to a powerful Roman governor named Pontius Pilate. Pilate asked Jesus, "Are you the King of the Jews?" Jesus answered, "My kingdom is not of this world. If my kingdom were of this world, my servants would fight so that I would not be delivered over to death."

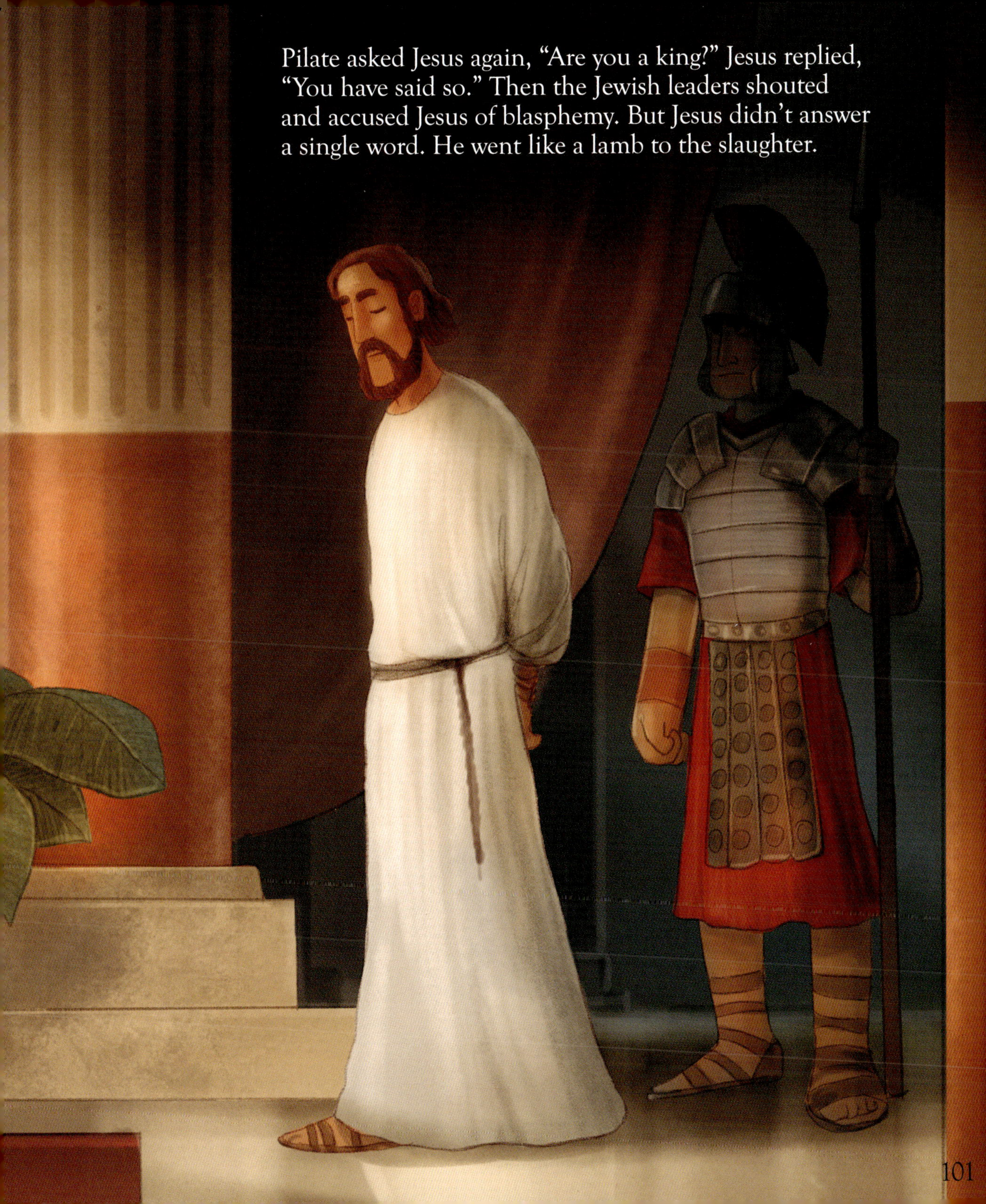

Pilate asked Jesus again, "Are you a king?" Jesus replied, "You have said so." Then the Jewish leaders shouted and accused Jesus of blasphemy. But Jesus didn't answer a single word. He went like a lamb to the slaughter.

Pilate handed Jesus over to Roman soldiers, and they whipped him.
The creator of all men was beaten and bruised by them.
His own people—the people of Israel—shouted and screamed for his death.
Jesus bore it all so that his people could be saved.

The soldiers twisted a crown of thorns and dressed him in a purple robe. They struck him and mocked him, saying, "Hail, King of the Jews!"

Pilate brought Jesus out before the Jews and said, “Behold your King!” The leaders of the Jews shouted, “Crucify him! He must die, because he claimed to be the Son of God.”

Pilate brought out a criminal and murderer named Barabbas. He offered the people a choice: “Should I let Jesus or Barabbas go free?” The crowds shouted, “Away with this man—release Barabbas to us!”

Pilate asked, “Shall I crucify your King?” The chief priests answered, “We have no king but Caesar.” So Pilate delivered Jesus over to be crucified. And he said, “I wash my hands of this.”

Jesus was forced to carry his cross outside of Jerusalem to a place called Golgotha. The soldiers drove nails into his hands and feet and raised him up on the cross. Above the cross they placed a sign. It read, "Jesus of Nazareth, the King of the Jews."
They were mocking him; they didn't really believe he was the King.

The Jewish leaders also mocked Jesus. They said, "He saved others, but he can't save himself. If he is really the King of Israel, let him come down from the cross and we will believe in him."

Jesus could have saved himself.
He could have called an army of angels
to deliver him and destroy all his enemies.
But Jesus hung there on the cross,
dying for his people. He called out,
"Father, forgive them, for they do not know
what they are doing."

Though it was the middle of the day, the sun went dark.
Jesus cried out, "My God, my God, why have you forsaken me?"

For all eternity, Jesus had perfect fellowship with his Father.
He had never known a moment apart from God's loving gaze.
But on the cross, Jesus was forsaken by God.
He bore his people's sin, so that they would never be forsaken.

Two criminals hung on the crosses beside Jesus.
One of them mocked Jesus, but the other believed.
He asked Jesus, "Remember me when you come into your kingdom."

At last, Jesus cried out, "It is finished!"
And he bowed his head and gave up his spirit.

When Jesus died, there was a great earthquake.
The curtain in the temple was torn in two from the top down.
This curtain symbolized the separation between
God's holiness and humanity's sinfulness. Through his death,
Jesus opened up a way into the Holy of holies—into God's very presence.
Jesus fulfilled God's covenant promises,
so that through faith we can enter into his kingdom.

Crowning the King

God's Presence: The veil in the Holy of holies being torn in two is one of the greatest moments in history. Through his death, Jesus has made a way for all people to enter into God's presence.

God's People: The people who should have rejoiced at the arrival of their promised King instead turn against him and demand that he be crucified. God made promises to Israel for thousands of years, but most of the Israelites rejected Jesus.

God's Place: On Mount Golgotha, Jesus is enthroned as King. Through his death, Jesus bridges the gap between heaven and earth. He makes a way for his people to enter into God's kingdom.

God's Promise: Jesus establishes the New Covenant through his crucifixion. He takes on the penalty of sin and death, so his people can have forgiveness and life.

Questions

1. Why did the Israelites demand that Jesus be crucified?
2. How did Jesus pay for our sins?
3. What was the significance of the veil in the Temple being torn?

Gospel Glimpse

2 Corinthians 5:21 says, "For our sake he made him to be sin who knew no sin, so that in him we might become the righteousness of God." Jesus is the substitute for our sin (1 John 2:2). Jesus paid the penalty for our sin once and for all (Hebrews 10:11-12).

Prayer

We praise you, our Lord, for making a way for us to come boldly before your throne of grace. We rejoice in the salvation you have given.

Chapter 9:
The King's Commission

Bible References:

Matthew 28, Luke 24

After Jesus died, some of his disciples took him down from the cross. They wrapped him in clean linen and laid him in a tomb. It seemed that all their hopes and dreams lay there cold and dead with Jesus' lifeless body.

They had hoped he would be the King who would set them free. They dreamed that Jesus would set up his kingdom on earth. But it seemed like evil had won, and that good would never rise again.

Jesus's disciples forgot what he promised: "After three days I will rise."
But the Jewish leaders remembered, and they wanted to make sure
no one would make up a story about Jesus rising from the dead.
They sealed the tomb with a heavy stone,
and placed soldiers there to guard it.

Three days later, two women rose early to go to Jesus' tomb.
As they approached the tomb, the sun rose in the distance—
lighting up the cold darkness of the night.

Suddenly, there was a great earthquake.
An angel of the Lord came down to roll back the stone.
The angel looked like a big flash of lightning;
his clothing was bright white.
The guards at the tomb were terrified and fainted!

The angel said to the women, "Do not be afraid,
for I know you seek Jesus who was crucified.
He is not here, for he has risen, as he said."

Later that day, two of the disciples were walking on a road to a village called Emmaus. A man joined them and asked, "What are you talking about?" They told him, "Have you not heard? Jesus of Nazareth was crucified three days ago. But we were hoping that he was the promised Savior who would redeem Israel."

The man told them, "O foolish ones, and slow to believe what the prophets have promised! Was it not necessary that the Savior should suffer these things before entering into his glory?" Then he showed them how all of the Old Testament was pointing to Jesus.

They invited the man to stay in their house for the night. As he broke bread for the meal, suddenly they recognized him—it was Jesus!

Now they understood all that Jesus had promised. Jesus truly was the promised Savior, bringing God's kingdom to this world.

Jesus appeared to many of his followers in the forty days after his resurrection. Then he prepared to leave them. The disciples met Jesus on a mountain in Galilee and worshiped him there. But some still doubted.

Jesus told them, “All authority in heaven and on earth has been given to me. Go therefore and make disciples of all nations, baptizing them in the name of the Father and of the Son and of the Holy Spirit, teaching them to obey all that I have commanded you. And behold, I am with you always, even to the end of the age.”

Long ago, God told Adam and Eve to be fruitful and multiply, and to fill the earth with people. Now Jesus gave his disciples a greater commission: to fill the earth with followers of Jesus!

Even after all this time, the disciples still didn't fully understand how God's kingdom would come. Some of them asked Jesus, "Lord, will you now restore the kingdom to Israel?"

He said to them, "It is not for you to know the times or seasons that the Father has determined. But you will receive power when the Holy Spirit has come upon you, and you will be my witnesses in Jerusalem and in all Judea and Samaria, and to the end of the earth."

Jesus was carried up on a cloud and ascended into heaven. God would empower his people through the Holy Spirit to tell the whole world about Jesus–the risen King!

The King's Commission

God's Presence: Jesus is raised from the dead by the power of God! When Jesus ascends into heaven, he promises his followers that he will be with them until the end of the age.

God's People: Now the disciples become God's messengers to proclaim the good news of God's kingdom to the world. Anyone who comes to Jesus in faith is joined into God's family.

God's Place: Jesus declares that he has all authority in heaven and on earth. By his resurrection, he demonstrated that he is Lord over everything. He commissions his disciples to go to the ends of the earth, because he is the King over all the earth.

God's Promise: God is fulfilling his promise to Abraham. Through Jesus, God will bring his blessing to all nations. People from every part of the world will be welcomed into God's kingdom through faith.

Questions

1. Why did the Pharisees place a stone over Jesus' tomb?
2. What did Jesus tell the two men on the road to Emmaus?
3. How would the good news of God's kingdom spread to all nations?

Gospel Glimpse

The Son of God rose victorious as the conquering king over sin and death. Jesus bridged the gap between heaven and earth, and made a way for them to be united forever (1 Timothy 2:5). From the cross, Jesus declared his reign as the true king over all things (Matthew 28:18).

Prayer

O risen King, we praise you for your life, death, and resurrection.
Help us to spread the good news of your kingdom to the ends of the earth.

Chapter 10: The Kingdom Grows

Bible References:

Acts 1-4

Fifty days after the Passover feast, the Jews celebrated a festival called Pentecost. On this day, many of the disciples were together in Jerusalem. They were waiting for the Holy Spirit to come, as Jesus had promised them.

Suddenly they heard a sound like a mighty rushing wind. It filled the entire house they were in. Tongues of fire appeared above each of them. They were all filled with the Holy Spirit and began to speak in other languages.

Just as God's presence had filled
the temple many years before,
believers were now filled with God's Spirit.
God was equipping them to be his messengers,
so that the good news of his kingdom
could reach to the ends of the earth.

Jews from every nation on earth were gathered in Jerusalem for Pentecost. They heard the Christians speaking of God's mighty works in many languages. They were amazed and said, "What does this mean?"

Peter told them, "Let all Israel know that God has made him both Lord and Christ—this Jesus whom you crucified." Peter told the Jews that Jesus was the promised Savior who they had been waiting for.

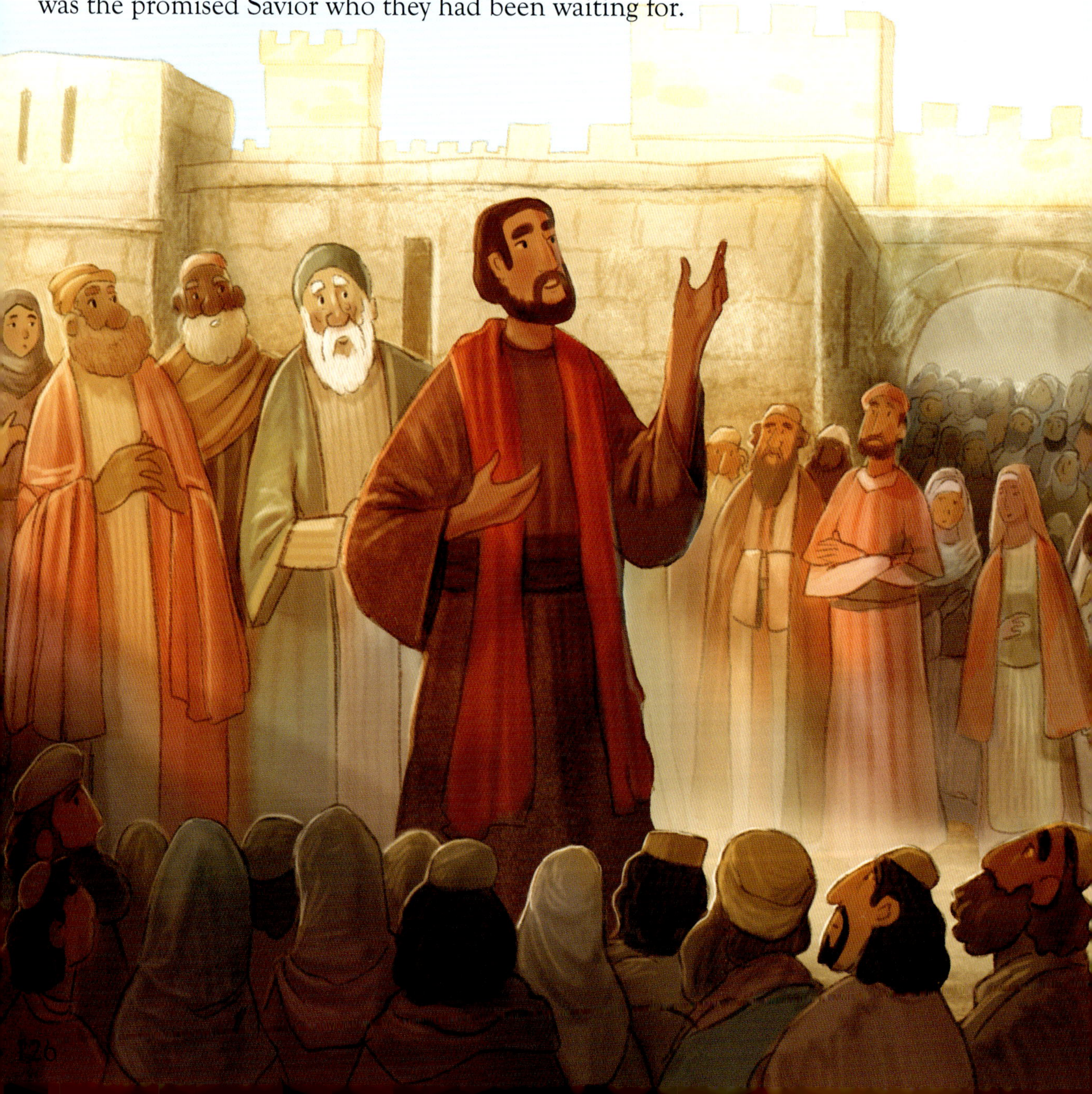

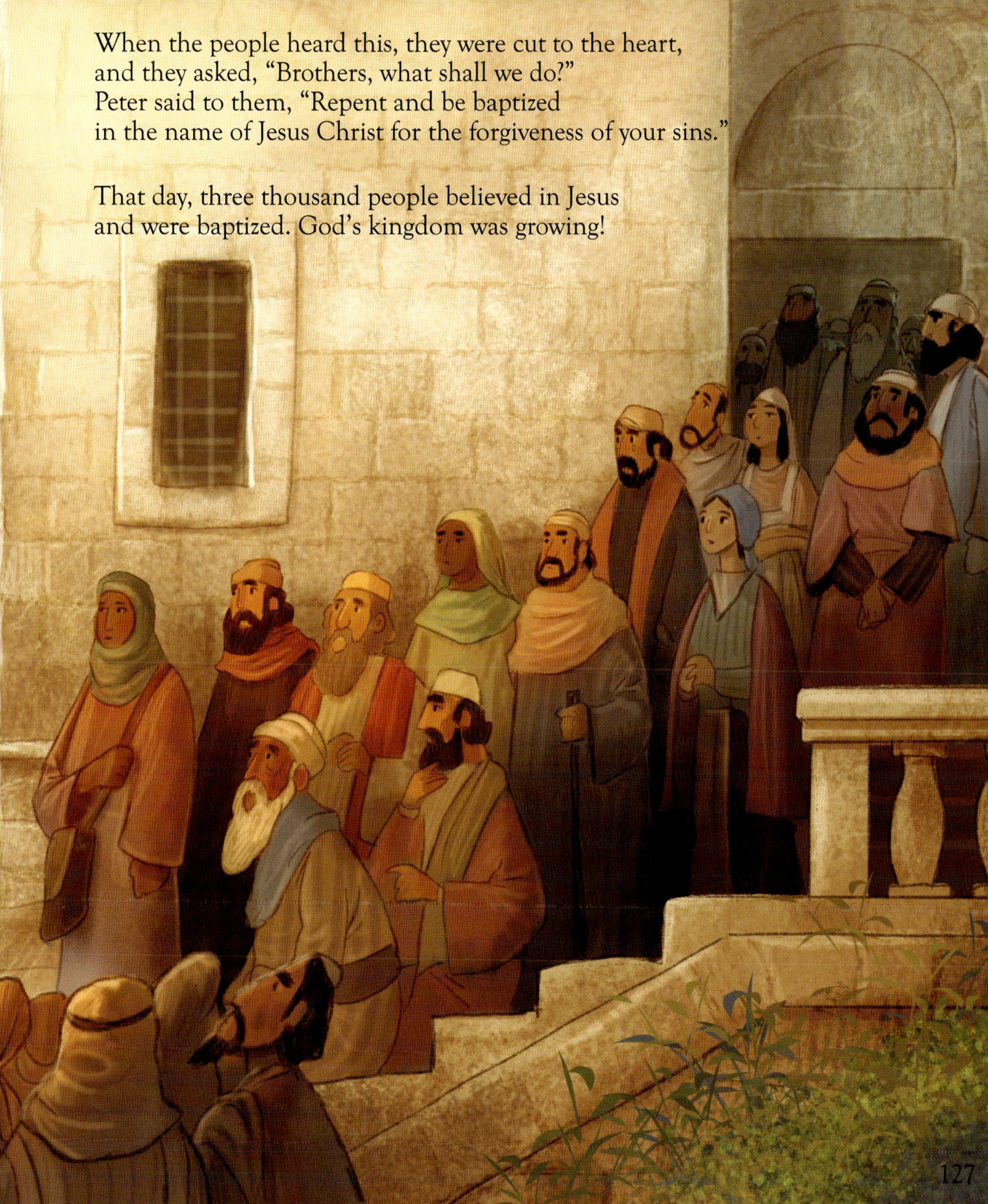

When the people heard this, they were cut to the heart,
and they asked, “Brothers, what shall we do?”
Peter said to them, “Repent and be baptized
in the name of Jesus Christ for the forgiveness of your sins.”

That day, three thousand people believed in Jesus
and were baptized. God’s kingdom was growing!

The Jewish leaders were angry that the church was growing. They wanted the apostles to stop preaching, so they arrested Peter and put him in prison. They told him, "Stop preaching about Jesus!"

That night, an angel of the Lord opened the prison doors and freed Peter. The angel told him, "Go to the temple and speak the words of life to the people."

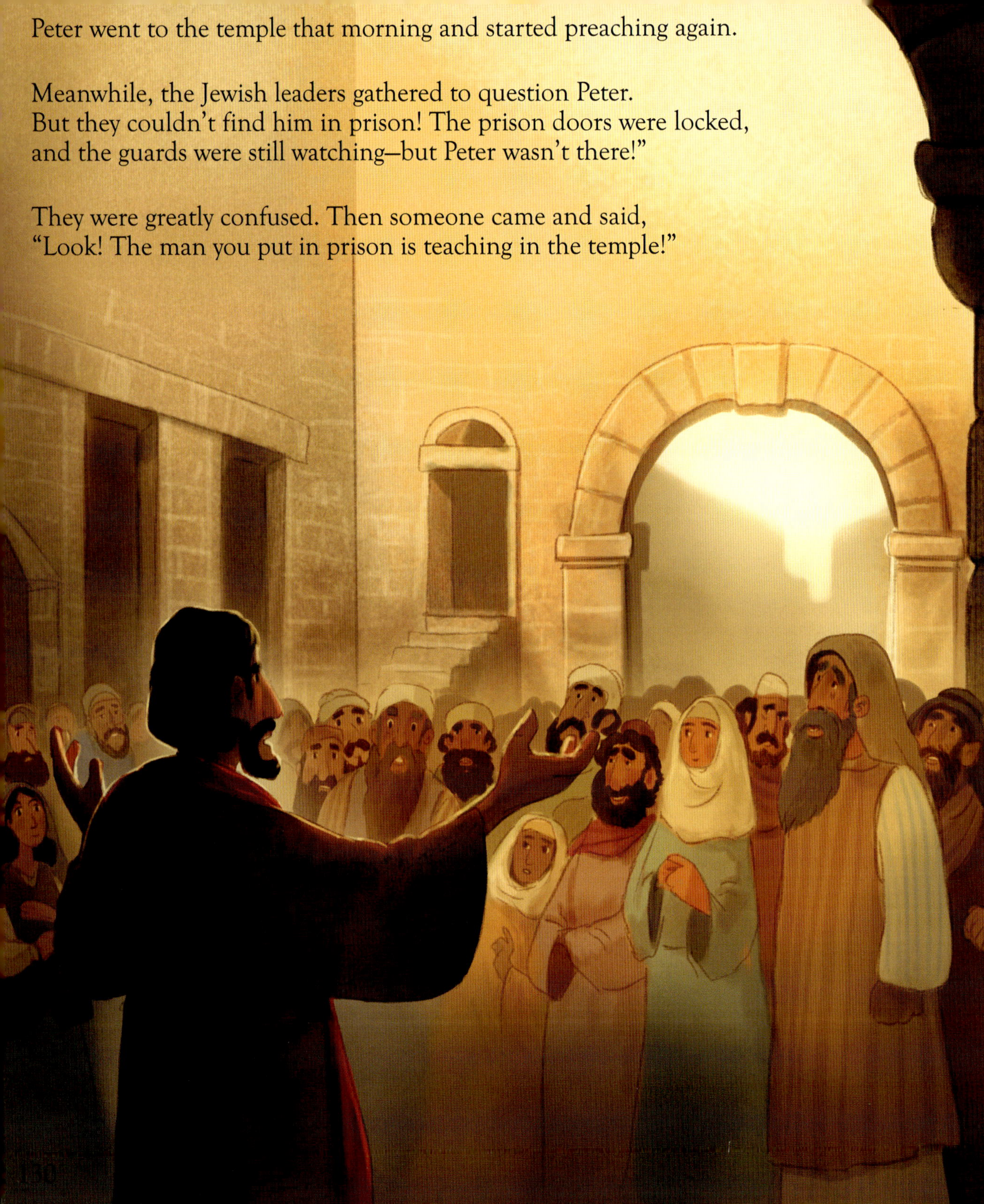

Peter went to the temple that morning and started preaching again.

Meanwhile, the Jewish leaders gathered to question Peter. But they couldn't find him in prison! The prison doors were locked, and the guards were still watching—but Peter wasn't there!"

They were greatly confused. Then someone came and said, "Look! The man you put in prison is teaching in the temple!"

They brought Peter before the Jewish council and said to him, "We commanded you to not preach about Jesus, but now you have filled Jerusalem with your teaching!"

Peter responded, "We cannot stop speaking of what we have seen and heard. We must obey God rather than men!"

When Peter was released, he joined the other believers and prayed: "Lord, help your servants to speak with all boldness."

Many people were amazed by the church and the signs and wonders being done by the apostles. The Christians devoted themselves to the apostles' teaching, to fellowship with one another, to breaking of bread, and to prayer. They gave generously to anyone in the church who had a need.

The kingdom of God continued to grow and flourish as the Holy Spirit empowered God's people to speak boldly about Jesus. It was an exciting time as the church was born—but things were about to get much more difficult.

The Kingdom Grows

God's Presence: The Holy Spirit fills believers and enables them to fulfill Jesus' commission. God's presence now dwells within his people through the Spirit, and Christians are considered the temple of God.

God's People: In the New Covenant, God's people are those who turn from their sin and trust in Jesus for their salvation. Everyone who puts their faith in Jesus is filled with the Holy Spirit.

God's Place: The church is the place where God reigns and where God's kingdom is put on display. All Christians are part of the universal church, which is the Bride of Christ.

God's Promise: Many prophecies of the New Covenant promised that God would put his Spirit inside believers. The Holy Spirit enables us to live as the people of God and to proclaim the kingdom of God.

Questions

1. Why did the Christians wait for the Holy Spirit to come?
2. How did Peter respond to threats from the religious leaders?
3. What did the early church devote themselves to?

Gospel Glimpse

Though Jesus ascended into heaven, he promised that he would send the Holy Spirit to help his people (John 14:16). The Holy Spirit now helps us to share the Gospel with boldness (2 Timothy 1:7), and to bear fruit as God's people (Galatians 5:22-23).

Prayer

Thank you, God, that your kingdom continues to grow as many place their faith in Jesus. We praise you for the gift of the Holy Spirit.

Chapter 11: A Kingdom of All Nations

Bible References:

Acts 6-10

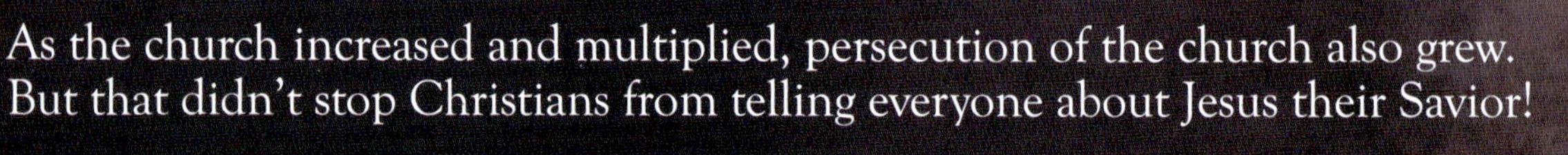

As the church increased and multiplied, persecution of the church also grew. But that didn't stop Christians from telling everyone about Jesus their Savior!

When a man named Stephen preached about Jesus, the Jewish leaders became furious. They tried to argue with him, but he was full of God's Spirit and had great wisdom. He told them, "You are just like your fathers! Which of the prophets did your fathers not persecute?" Just as the Israelites had rejected so many prophets, the Jewish leaders were rejecting Jesus.

Stephen looked up and said, “I see the heavens opened, and the Son of Man standing at the right hand of God.” Then they shouted at him and rushed at him. They cast Stephen out of the city and stoned him. As he died, Stephen called out, “Lord Jesus, receive my spirit.” And falling to his knees, he cried out, “Lord, do not hold this sin against them.”

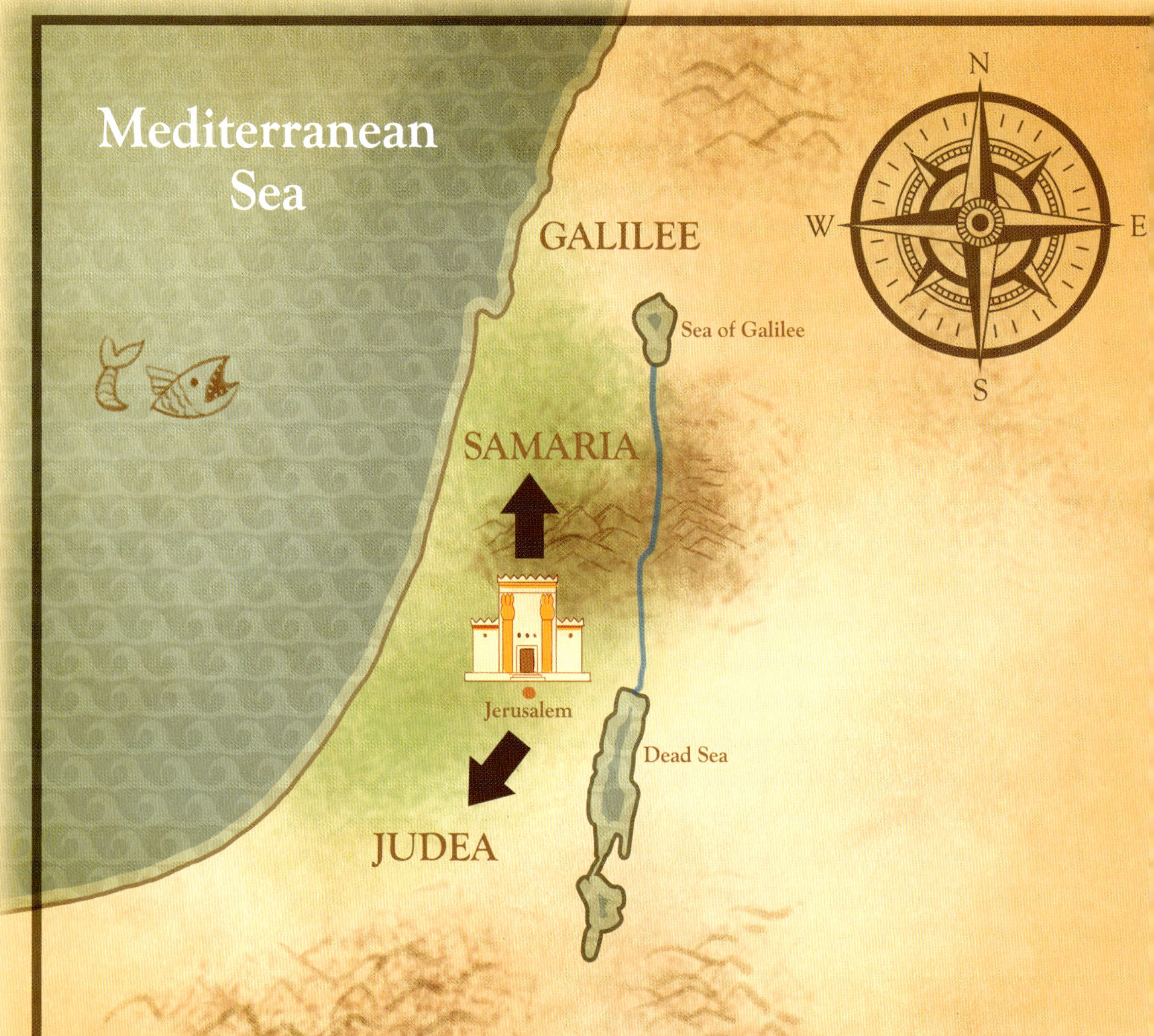

After Stephen's death, a great persecution arose against Christians. Jesus' followers were scattered throughout Judea and Samaria. Wherever they went, they shared the gospel. Evil men tried to stop this, but God's kingdom could not be stopped. It just kept growing! Jesus kept building his church through the power of the Holy Spirit.

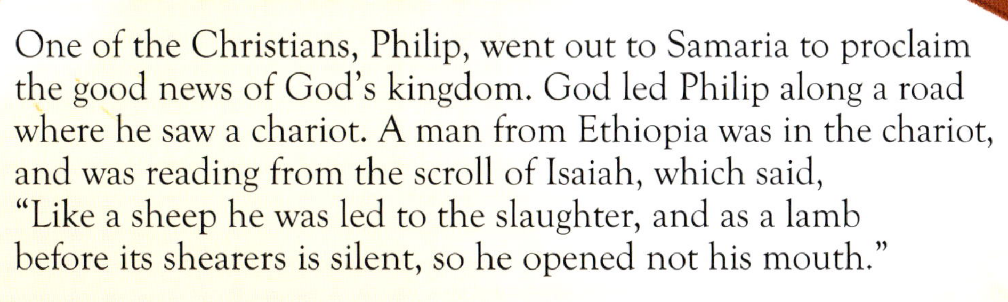

One of the Christians, Philip, went out to Samaria to proclaim the good news of God's kingdom. God led Philip along a road where he saw a chariot. A man from Ethiopia was in the chariot, and was reading from the scroll of Isaiah, which said, "Like a sheep he was led to the slaughter, and as a lamb before its shearers is silent, so he opened not his mouth."

The man asked Philip, "Who is this speaking about?" And Philip told him, "This is about Jesus!" The man believed and was baptized that same day. God was bringing people from all over the world into his kingdom.

Some of the Jewish Christians couldn't understand God's plan to save people from every nation. They thought people from other nations were outsiders and didn't belong in God's kingdom.

This has always been difficult for God's people to understand. Hundreds of years before, God called Jonah to preach to the town of Nineveh. Jonah couldn't believe it! The Ninevites were one of Israel's worst enemies. It took getting swallowed up by a fish to convince him to go.

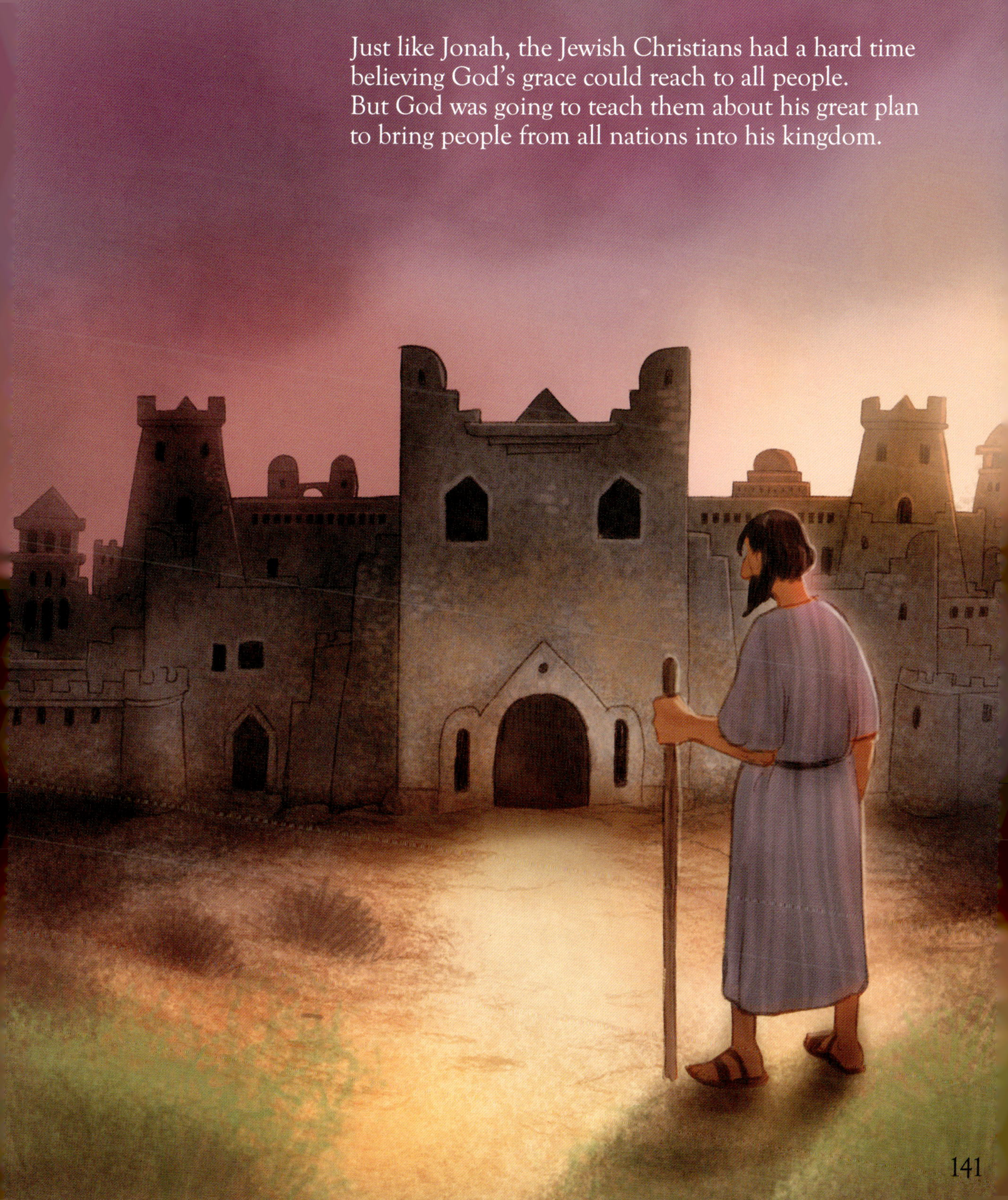

Just like Jonah, the Jewish Christians had a hard time believing God's grace could reach to all people. But God was going to teach them about his great plan to bring people from all nations into his kingdom.

Even the apostle Peter was slow to believe God's plan.
One day, Peter went up to his roof to pray. God showed Peter a vision of a great sheet coming down from heaven. It was filled with all kinds of animals that a Jew would never eat.

In the Old Testament, some animals were considered unclean.
There were many laws about which foods a Jew could not eat.

God told Peter, “Rise and eat.” But Peter said, “I have never eaten anything common or unclean.” Then God said, “What God has made clean, do not call unclean.”

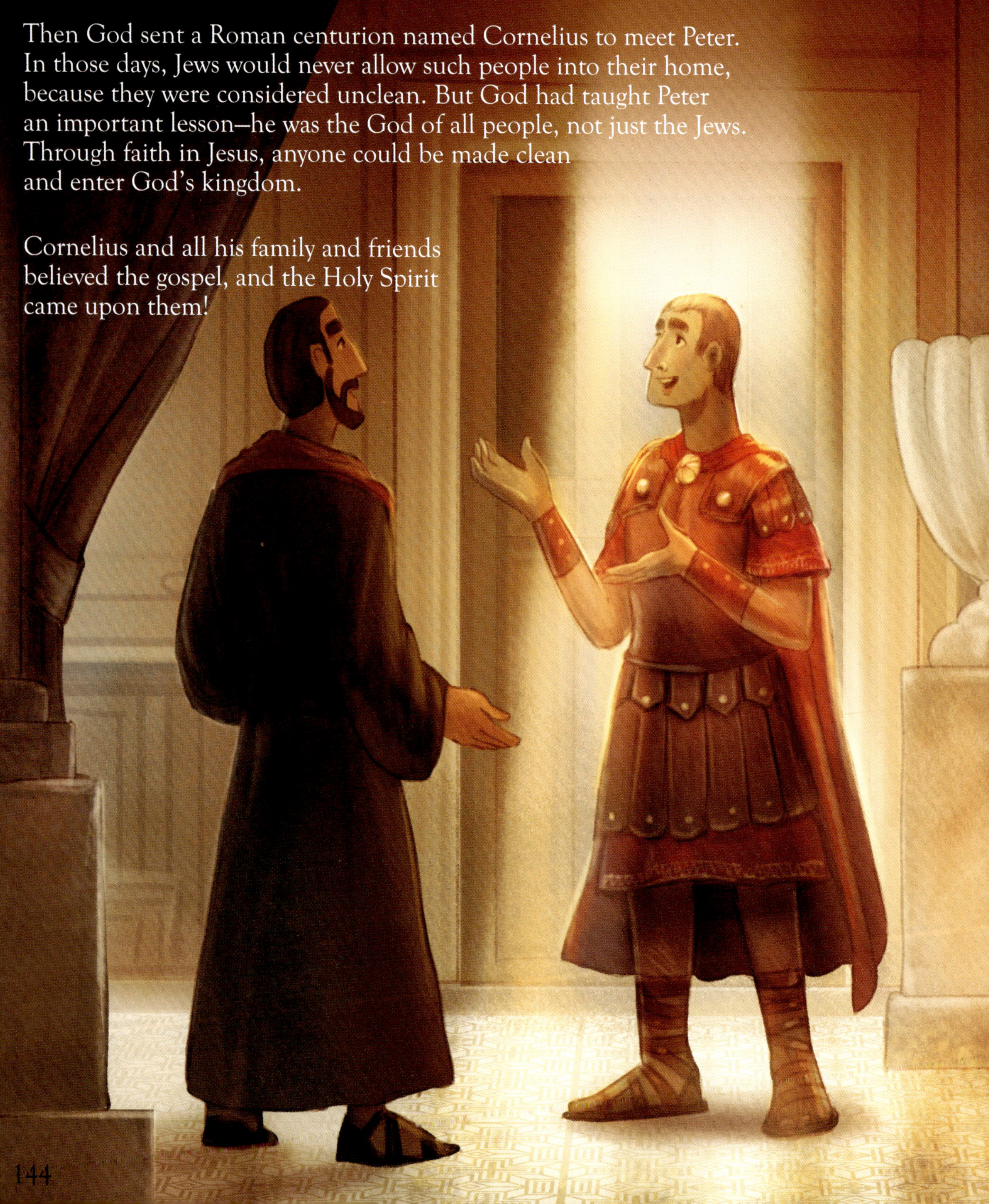

Then God sent a Roman centurion named Cornelius to meet Peter. In those days, Jews would never allow such people into their home, because they were considered unclean. But God had taught Peter an important lesson—he was the God of all people, not just the Jews. Through faith in Jesus, anyone could be made clean and enter God's kingdom.

Cornelius and all his family and friends believed the gospel, and the Holy Spirit came upon them!

The word of God increased and multiplied—not just to the Jews, but to Judea, and Samaria, and to the ends of the earth. God's plan to bless all nations through Jesus was beginning, and it would only grow more and more.

A Kingdom of All Nations

God's Presence: Stephen sees Jesus standing beside God's throne. Jesus is with his people as they face difficulties. The Holy Spirit fills the Gentile believers, which shows how God is bringing people from all nations into his kingdom.

God's People: The Jews were God's chosen people, and they were slow to understand God's plan to extend salvation to the Gentiles. God demonstrates that he is the God of all nations, and uses his people to spread this good news to the ends of the earth.

God's Place: The Christians are scattered throughout Judea and Samaria. Through this difficult time, God is using his people to spread the message of his kingdom to other nations.

God's Promise: The Holy Spirit filling the Gentiles is the fulfillment of God's many promises to bring his salvation to all nations. It also enables the Jewish Christians to understand the global nature of God's kingdom.

Questions

1. Why were the Christians scattered to Judea and Samaria?
2. How were Peter and Jonah similar?
3. What was the significance of the Holy Spirit filling the Gentiles?

Gospel Glimpse

Many of the prophets spoke of a day when people from all over the world would worship God (Isaiah 19:23). The promised Savior would be a light to all the nations (Isaiah 49:6). Jesus is the promised offspring of Abraham who brings God's blessing to the world (Genesis 12:3).

Prayer

O God, you are the king of all nations. We pray the Gospel would spread the very ends of the earth, so that many can find salvation in Jesus.

Chapter 12:
Building the Kingdom

Bible References:

Acts 9, Acts 14-28

One of the people who tried the hardest to stop the church
was a Jewish leader named Saul. He carefully studied the Old Testament,
but he refused to see how all the prophets pointed to Jesus.
He did not believe Jesus was the promised Savior,
and wanted to make sure no one preached about Jesus.

Saul made it his mission to destroy the church. He traveled to many towns and went from house to house searching for followers of Jesus. He dragged many Christians into jail, and threatened to kill anyone who believed in Jesus.

Saul went to Damascus to persecute more of Jesus's followers.
As Saul traveled on the road, a bright light from heaven suddenly shone around him. Saul fell to the ground.
He heard a voice saying, "Saul, Saul, why are you persecuting me?"

Saul asked, "Who are you, Lord?" And the voice responded, "I am Jesus, the one you are persecuting."

Saul became blind for three days, until God restored his sight. Now Saul could see that Jesus truly was the promised Savior!

Before God saved him, Saul tried to destroy the church with great zeal. Now he would build the church with even greater zeal. Saul came to be known as Paul, and he traveled throughout many regions as a missionary.

Through the power of the Holy Spirit, Paul spoke boldly in the synagogues, convincing other Jews that Jesus was the promised Savior. Paul showed them how the whole Old Testament was pointing to Jesus.

God also called Paul to bring the gospel
to many other nations.
Now these people were being saved
and forming their own churches.
Just as Jesus promised, God's kingdom
was expanding to the ends of the earth!

As Paul traveled, he faced great persecution.
Many Jews still refused to believe that Jesus was God's Son.
And many Romans didn't believe that there was only one true God.

When Paul and his friend Silas were preaching in Philippi, some of the people became angry with them. They brought these men before the rulers and said, "These men are Jews, and they are disturbing our city. They teach things that are not lawful for us to accept."

Paul and Silas were beaten with rods and thrown into prison.
The jailer locked their feet in chains.

Instead of being sad or discouraged by this, Paul and Silas sang hymns! At about midnight a great earthquake shook the prison and all the prisoners' chains came undone!

The jailer woke up and saw the prison doors were opened. He thought everyone had escaped and knew he would be in big trouble. But Paul called out, "Do not harm yourself! We are all still here."

The jailer rushed in and fell before Paul and Silas and said, "What must I do to be saved?" And Paul told him, "Believe in the Lord Jesus, and you will be saved."

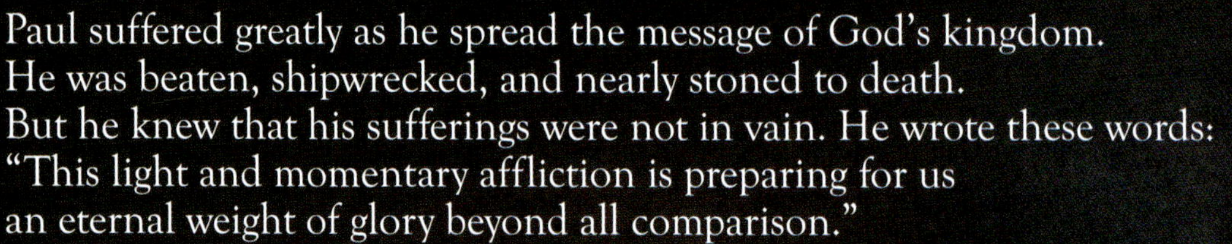
Paul suffered greatly as he spread the message of God's kingdom.
He was beaten, shipwrecked, and nearly stoned to death.
But he knew that his sufferings were not in vain. He wrote these words:
"This light and momentary affliction is preparing for us
an eternal weight of glory beyond all comparison."

Paul would spend much of his ministry in prison for preaching the gospel.
But God's Word is too powerful to be bound by chains or prison cells.
The Holy Spirit inspired Paul to write many letters while he was in prison.
God used these letters to build up his church.

Despite all the difficulties he faced, Paul remained steadfast, because he had a hope laid up in heaven. Paul told the church: “The Lord will rescue me from every evil deed and bring me safely into his heavenly kingdom. To him be the glory forever and ever.”

Building the Kingdom

God's Presence: God chose to supernaturally intervene in Paul's life and transform him. God continues to work in many lives today, transforming people by the power of the Holy Spirit.

God's People: Paul spent his whole life studying the Old Testament, but was still blind to the truth that Jesus is the Promised Savior. It is only through faith in Jesus that someone can become one of God's people.

God's Place: Paul was persecuting the church, but Jesus asks him, "Why are you persecuting me?" Jesus is the head of the church, and the church is now God's place on this earth. He is working in the midst of his people.

God's Promise: Jesus promised to build his church, and he would build it in many surprising ways. Even persecution and difficulty helped to grow the church.

Questions

1. Why was Paul persecuting the church?
2. How did God transform Paul?
3. What hope did Paul have in his suffering?

Gospel Glimpse

God is able to change the hardest heart through the Holy Spirit, just as he changed Paul's heart (2 Corinthians 4:6). Though we were dead in sin, God makes us alive in Christ (Ephesians 2:5).

Prayer

God, your grace is amazing. Thank you for giving us eyes to see that Jesus is the only Savior. Help us to build your kingdom by sharing this good news.

Chapter 13: The Kingdom on Earth

Bible References:

Romans 6, 1 Corinthians 11, Ephesians 6

Most of the New Testament is made of letters written to growing churches. These letters were inspired by God's Spirit and became part of God's Word. They helped Christians understand how they were to think and live as citizens of God's kingdom.

In a letter to the Ephesians church, Paul explained, "You are members of the household of God. In Jesus you are being built together into a dwelling place for God by the Spirit."

Through Jesus, everyone was welcome into the church. Christians are now called the temple of God. Just as God's presence once dwelled in the temple, so God now lives and works in his people.

Baptism is a powerful symbol of this new life in Jesus. When a person is placed into the water, it represents how they have died to their old way of life in sin and rebellion. When they rise, it represents how they have been raised to new spiritual life with Christ.

Baptism is an outward sign of an inward reality.
We have been cleansed from sin and are now citizens of God's kingdom!
Paul wrote to the Colossian church, saying, "God has delivered us from the domain of darkness and brought us into the kingdom of his beloved Son."

Sharing communion, or the Lord's Supper, is another symbol God has given to the church. It helps us to remember all that Jesus has done and will do. The bread represents Jesus body, and the cup represents his blood. We take communion to remember the great sacrifice Jesus made for us on the cross.

But we also eat it to look forward to the day that Jesus will return. Paul told the churches, "For as often as you eat this bread and drink the cup, you proclaim the Lord's death until he comes."

A great and glorious day is coming when we will share a feast with Jesus in heaven. We will join in the marriage supper of the Lamb as we are united with Christ forever.

Jesus has already won the victory over Satan, but Christians still live in a spiritual war. Just as Satan tried to deceive God's people in the past, he continues to wage war against the church.

How can we stand against such a powerful enemy? Not in our own strength, but through the armor of God! Paul told the Ephesian church, "Be strong in the Lord and in the strength of his might. Put on the whole armor of God, that you may be able to stand against the schemes of the devil."

Christians must put on the belt of truth, the breastplate of righteousness, the shoes of the gospel of peace, the shield of faith, the helmet of salvation, and the sword of the Spirit.

We can have victory over Satan because Jesus was victorious!
By the power of God's Spirit,
we can stand firm against our enemy.
God has promised that one day
he will crush Satan underneath our feet!

Jesus is the head of the church, and we are his body here on earth. When we live out our calling as Christians, we are given a glimpse of God's kingdom on this earth. We show the world what it looks like to live under God's reign through our words and actions.

We are God's messengers. He has called us to spread the Gospel to the ends of the earth. We gather in the church to worship our King, and then we scatter into the world welcome others into God's kingdom.

The Kingdom on Earth

God's Presence: Christians are united with Christ and filled with the Holy Spirit. God is working in and through his church to put his kingdom on display to the world.

God's People: Like Israel lived in exile in Babylon, Christians are strangers and exiles in this world. We are citizens of heaven waiting for our King to establish his kingdom on earth.

God's Place: All Christians are part of the body of Christ, which is the universal church. But Christians are also called to be part of a local church, which God has planted throughout all the world.

God's Promise: We live each day knowing that Jesus is with us and will never forsake us. We look forward in hope for the day that Jesus will come again and establish his eternal kingdom.

Questions

1. What does baptism represent?
2. Why is communion important?
3. How will the message of God's kingdom spread to the earth?

Gospel Glimpse

Everyone who turns from their sin and trusts in Jesus is united with him (Galatians 2:20). We are clothed in Christ's righteousness and given a new identity as sons and daughters of the King (1 John 3:1).

Prayer

We praise you, O God, for giving us the church to strengthen and equip us for our life in this world.

Chapter 14: The Conquering King

Bible References:

Revelation 1-5, Revelation 5:9-10

As time went on, many of the apostles died for their faith, and many Christians suffered rejection from family and neighbors. The apostle John was the last apostle to die. The Roman emperor didn't want John to preach anymore, so he was exiled to an island called Patmos.

While John was there, God gave him a vision of what would happen in the future. God wanted his people to know that no matter how hard things became, one day his kingdom would come. Even if the church felt small and defeated in a world full of evil, God was still on his throne and still guiding all of history.

John saw Jesus in his vision, reigning in glory and shining like the sun. Jesus told John, "Fear not, I am the first and the last, and the living one. I died, and behold I am alive forevermore!"

John heard a voice call out to him, "Come up here. I will show you what must soon take place." John was taken up into heaven's throne room. He saw God sitting on his throne as King over the universe. There was a brilliant light behind the throne, and flashes of lightning and thunder. In front of the throne was a sea of glass.

On each side of God's throne were angelic beings with six wings. Day and night they continually praised God saying, "Holy, holy, holy is the Lord God Almighty, who was and is and is to come!"

John saw twenty-four elders bowing before God's throne. They cast their crowns down before the throne, saying, "Worthy are you, our Lord and God, to receive glory and power!"

God held a scroll that was sealed with seven seals.
This scroll held God's plans for the future–
his plans to bring in his kingdom
and to defeat all evil in the world.

A mighty angel called out, "Who is worthy to open the scroll
or look inside it?" No one in heaven or on earth was found
who was able to open the scroll or look inside it.
So John began to weep.

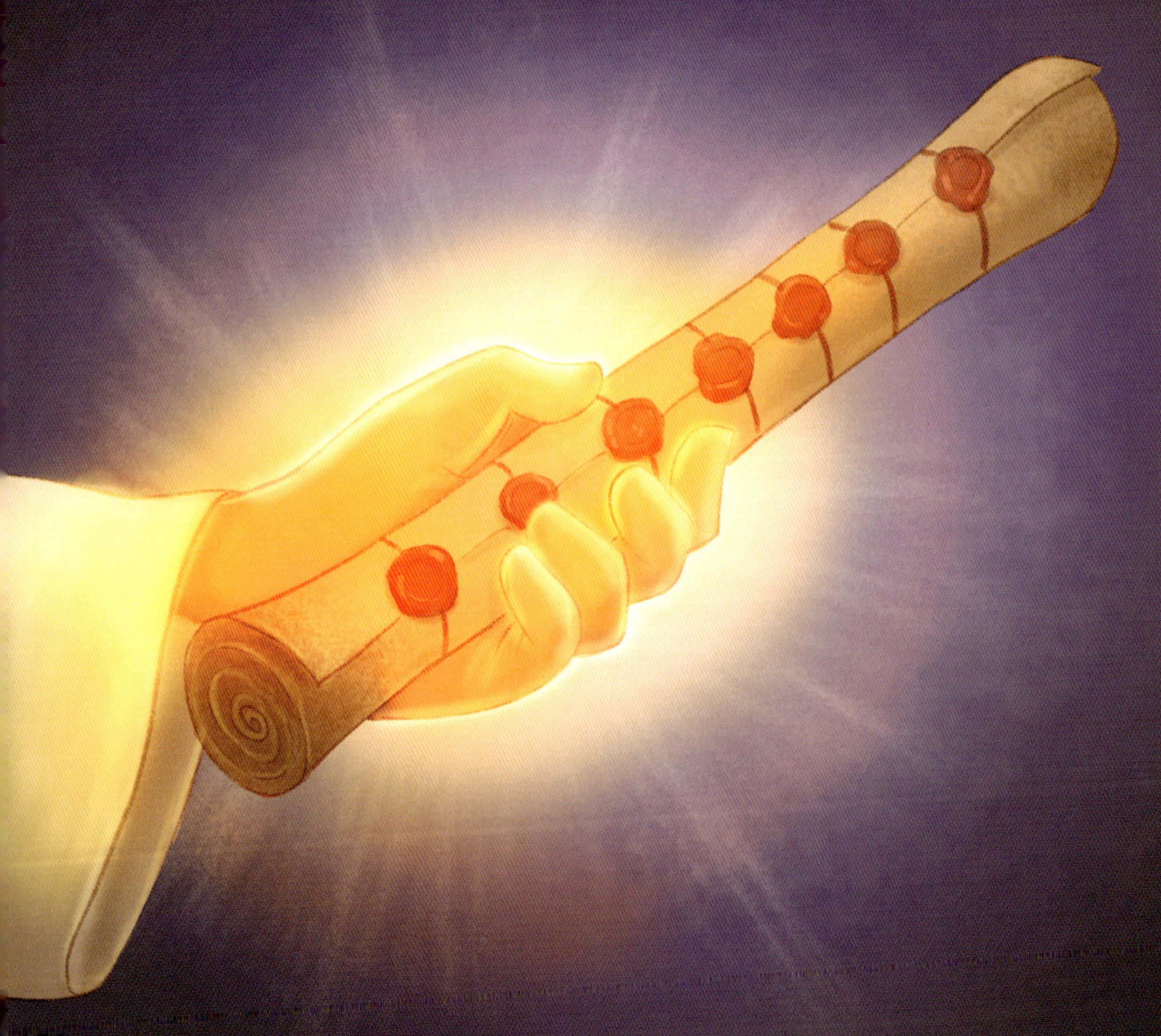

Then an elder called out, "Weep no more! Behold, the Lion of the tribe of Judah, the Root of David, has conquered. He can open the scroll and its seven seals." When John looked up, he saw a lamb standing as if it had been slain. Jesus was the conquering lion and the sacrificial lamb! He alone could open the scroll!

Everyone in heaven sang out, "Worthy are you to take the scroll and to open its seals, for you were slain, and by your blood you purchased people for God. You have made them a kingdom and priests to our God, and they will reign on the earth."

As God began to unfold his plans for the future, everyone in heaven broke out in praise—people from all nations of the earth from all times in history. They all gathered around the throne and worshiped Jesus, singing, “Worthy is the lamb who was slain!”

There were loud voices in heaven proclaiming:
"The kingdom of the world has become the kingdom of our Lord and of his Christ, and he will reign forever and ever."

Then John saw heaven open and a rider on a white horse rode out of the clouds. On his robe was written, "King of kings and Lord of lords."

There was a great war and all the forces of evil and darkness came to fight against Jesus and his army. But it wasn't really a battle, because Jesus conquered his enemies with his powerful word.

When Jesus first came to this world, he came in humility and weakness. He suffered and died for sin, and it seemed that he had been defeated. But when Jesus returns in power and glory as the conquering King, every knee will bow before him, and every tongue confess that he is Lord.

The Conquering King

God's Presence: Jesus walks among the seven lampstands, which are symbolic of the seven churches. This reminds God's people that Jesus is with them even in their difficulties. One day Jesus will return to earth and end all evil.

God's People: John is given a vision into the throne room of heaven, and he sees people from every tribe, tongue, nation, and language worshipping God around his throne. This is the fulfillment of God's plan from the beginning, that people from everywhere in the world would become part of his kingdom.

God's Place: Jesus will come as the conquering king to claim back all that is rightfully his. Every inch of the universe belongs to God, and by defeating death and sin he will establish his reign over everything.

God's Promise: Jesus alone is able to take the scroll and fulfill all of God's plans for the universe. Jesus will return and place all of God's enemies underneath his feet.

Questions

1. What does John see in his vision?
2. Why is Jesus able to open God's scroll?
3. How did Jesus defeat his enemies?

Gospel Glimpse

Jesus is both the lamb that was slain for our sins, and the lion that conquered death (Revelation 5:5-6). Jesus alone is worthy to fulfill all of God's plans for the future, and lead his people into his kingdom (Revelation 5:9-10).

Prayer

Lord Jesus, you are the conquering king! You have defeated death and sin. We praise you for making us your people.

Chapter 15: The Eternal Kingdom

Bible References:

Revelation 18-22, 1 Corinthians 15

John saw many great and glorious things in the visions God gave him. These visions showed that God would be victorious over all evil. John saw a vision of the great city of Babylon being destroyed. This city represented all the evil kingdoms of this world, all those who opposed God and persecuted God's people.

Ever since Adam and Eve sinned, people have rejected God's reign as King and tried to build their own kingdoms. In the end, all these false kingdoms will be destroyed, and God's kingdom alone will remain forever

John also saw a great white throne. Before the throne were all people, great and small. Books were opened, telling all the good and bad deeds people had ever done. Everyone was judged by what was written in the books.

But another book was there—the Book of Life!
It told the names of everyone who believed in Jesus.
Instead of facing eternal judgment,
they were given the gift of eternal life in God's kingdom!

Though John saw many visions of destruction on earth, he also saw the glorious plans God had for his people.

John saw a new Jerusalem coming down from heaven to earth. He heard a voice from God's throne call out, "Behold, the dwelling place of God is with man. He will dwell with them, and they will be his people, and God himself will be with them as their God. He will wipe away every tear from their eyes, and death will be no more. There will not be any mourning, or crying, or pain anymore, for the former things have passed away."

Everyone who trusts in Jesus will be welcomed into his kingdom—not because of what they've done, but because of what he did!

John heard God call out from his throne:
“Behold, I am making all things new!
It is done! I am the Alpha and the Omega,
the beginning and the end.
To the thirsty I will give from the spring
of the water of life without payment.”

John saw the river of the water of life flowing from God's throne
through the middle of the new Jerusalem.
And beside it, John saw the tree of life,
for healing the nations.

All of God's promises were coming true!
The new earth will be even better than Eden.
Like Adam and Eve, we'll be able to walk with God.
We will be given new bodies and new hearts that will always want to obey God, so we will never struggle with sin again.

The new earth will be even better than the promised land.
We'll never be sent away into exile like Israel was.
Nothing will ever separate us from God's love.

Best of all, John said this: "They will see God's face, and his name will be on their foreheads. And night will be no more. They will need no light from a lamp or the sun, for the Lord God will be their light, and they will reign forever and ever."

God's kingdom will come, on earth as it is in heaven. We will reign over the new earth as sons and daughters of God—the true and eternal King over all things.

At last, and forevermore: We will dwell in God's presence and delight in God's grace, as God's chosen people in God's promised place.

The Eternal Kingdom

God's Presence: In the amazing conclusion to the story of Redemption, John hears a voice call out, "Behold, the dwelling place of God is with man. He will dwell with them, and they will be his people." Like Eden, we will live in God's presence and not feel ashamed or afraid because of our sin.

God's People: Everyone who has their name written in the Book of Life will not face judgment but will be freely welcomed into God's kingdom. God will wipe away all tears from their eyes and call them to reign with Jesus forever.

God's Place: Heaven and earth will finally be united! The New Jerusalem will come down to the New Earth, and God will live with us. God's place will be our place and there will be no more sin or evil in the world.

God's Promise: We see all of God's glorious promises fulfilled as he builds his kingdom on earth. Everyone who trusts in Jesus and turns from their sin will receive the promise of eternal life with God. There will be no more darkness, or sadness, or sickness, or fear.

Questions

1. Who will face God's judgment at the Great White Throne?
2. How can we know we will be welcomed into God's kingdom?
3. What most excites you about the New Earth?

Gospel Glimpse

If we believe in Jesus as our Savior, our name is written in the book of life (Revelation 20:14-15). Instead of facing God's judgment, we will receive his grace forever (Ephesians 2:1-7).

Prayer

Come, Lord Jesus! We long for your return. We can't wait for the day you will restore all things and bring us into a new heaven and earth.

The Story Continues...

The story of the Bible is finished, but God continues to build his kingdom through his church. Though this world can seem sad and difficult some days, we have great hope in God’s promises. One day, all who believe in Jesus will rise from the dead so they can live forever in God's perfect kingdom.

Jesus promised to prepare a place for us so that we can be with him forever. We can only begin to imagine how great and glorious God’s kingdom will be. God will show the riches of his grace to us for all eternity. We will receive an eternal inheritance as God’s sons and daughters.

While we wait and long for Jesus to return, we are called to be God’s messengers. He has entrusted this good news to us, and calls us to invite many to join in his kingdom.

God's kingdom will come, and his will shall be done, on earth as it is in heaven. Jesus is coming soon! Amen, come King Jesus!

An Invitation

The Bible ends with this invitation into God's kingdom: "Let the one who hears say, 'Come.' And let the one who is thirsty come. Let the one who desires take the water of life without price." God is inviting you to come find true and eternal life!

We were made to dwell with God. He made us to live with him and reign with him in his kingdom. The Bible promises that Jesus will give a 'crown of righteousness' to everyone who longs and looks for his return (2 Timothy 4:8).

Our only hope of entering God's kingdom is through Jesus. The Bible says there is no way we could ever earn our place in God's kingdom. We have sinned. We've fallen short of God's plan. But Jesus has made a way for us through his life, death, and resurrection! He lived a perfect life, and died in our place to pay for our sins (2 Corinthians 5:21).

Have you received that invitation? It is a free gift of God's grace that can only be received by faith in Jesus (Ephesians 2:8-9).

Jesus Fulfills God's Covenants

The Covenant with Noah (Genesis 9:9-17)

Jesus takes the judgment that our sin deserves, so we can enter into God's kingdom and receive his grace.

The Covenant with Abraham (Genesis 12:1-3)

Jesus is the promised Offspring of Abraham who brings God's blessing to all the nations.

The Covenant with Israel (Exodus 19:1-8)

Jesus fully obeyed God's commands and fulfilled the law. He bore the curse of sin so that we can receive God's blessing.

The Covenant with David (2 Samuel 7:8-16)

Jesus is the promised son of David who reigns forever and establishes God's kingdom on earth.

The New Covenant (Jeremiah 31:31-34)

Jesus established the New Covenant in his blood. He made a way for anyone to receive the forgiveness of sins and new life.

More Books by Lithos Kids:

Little Pilgrim's Big Journey Part I & II are available now! Rediscover John Bunyan's timeless Christian tale, now beautifully illustrated and adapted for children ages 2-10 in heirloom quality books.

Lithos Kids exists to magnify Christ through biblically-faithul and beautifully-crafted books. Visit our website **LithosKids.com** to learn more about upcoming releases and purchase audiobooks.

Promises Made

The Kingdom of God Bible Storybook: Old Testament tells the beginning of the greatest story ever told. It sets the stage for the New Testament, and creates a longing for the promised King to come and restore God's kingdom to this broken world!

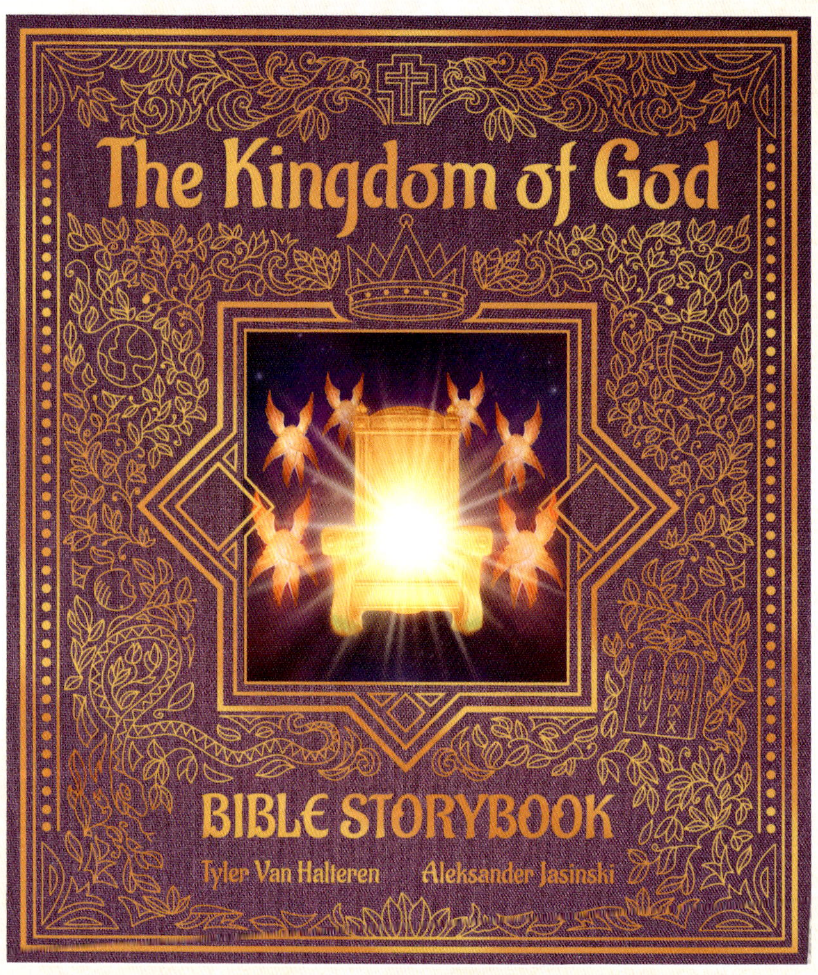